Search
for the
Navajo Code
Talkers

SEARCH FOR THE NAVAJO CODE TALKERS

SALLY MCCLAIN

Sally McClain

RIO NUEVO PUBLISHERS

Rio Nuevo Publishers®
P.O. Box 5250
Tucson, AZ 85703-0250
(520) 623-9558, www.rionuevo.com

See page 123 for photography credits.
Map © 2012 by Tom Jonas.
Book design: Rudy Ramos Design.
Cover design: David Jenney.

On the front cover and title page: George Willie Sr. salutes during ceremonies for Navajo
    Code Talker Day on August 14, 2009.
On the back cover: Carl Gorman, Window Rock, Arizona, 1986.

Printed in United States of America

10 9 8 7 6 5 4 3 2

Library of Congress Cataloging-in-Publication Data

McClain, S. (Sally)
  Search for the Navajo code talkers / Sally McClain.
     p. cm.
  Includes index.
   ISBN 978-1-933855-77-6 (pbk. : alk. paper) -- ISBN 1-933855-77-0 (pbk.
   : alk. paper)
1. World War, 1939-1945—Cryptography. 2. World War,
1939-1945—Participation, Indian. 3. Navajo language. 4. Navajo code
talkers. 5. United States—Armed Forces—Indian troops—History. I.
Title.
  D810.C88M383 2012
  940.54'8673--dc23
                         2012007828

To the Navajo Nation who nurtured the men who became the Marine Corps Navajo code talkers of World War II. To everyone who put on a uniform, worked in a factory, shipyard, or farm, endured deprivation, rationing, and the loss of a family member during a time when the whole world was wrapped in madness. I live a life of freedom and unlimited possibilities because of their sacrifice. I am what they fought and died for and I will always be grateful and I will never forget.

CONTENTS

Introduction 1

CHAPTER **1**: An Interesting Little Story 5

CHAPTER **2**: Harold Foster 9

CHAPTER **3**: Carl and Mary Gorman 21

CHAPTER **4**: "The One" 31

CHAPTER **5**: The First 29 35

CHAPTER **6**: The Archives 49

CHAPTER **7**: Questions and Answers 61

CHAPTER **8**: The Code Talkers Speak, Part 1 67

CHAPTER **9**: Extended Research 81

CHAPTER **10**: The Code Talkers Speak, Part 2 87

CHAPTER **11**: The Process Begins 103

Epilogue 115
Personal Notes 117
Acknowledgments 119
Suggested Reading 121
Photo Credits 123
Index 125
About the Author 128

Navajo Code Talkers Association, Window Rock, Arizona, 1994.

INTRODUCTION

NAVAJO WEAPON, my book about the Marine Corps Navajo code talkers of World War II, is one of the greatest accomplishments of my life. Next to having my daughter, it was the most wonderful adventure, from the beginning to the conclusion of the publication of their story. Over the last decade, a multitude of people have asked me how I came to this story and I have always had to give a very short version of the events that led me to these remarkable Native Americans. The explanation is more complex and complicated than a few cryptic sentences.

During this journey, I traveled into a world I was completely unfamiliar and unaware of and met the most incredible people I would ever have the privilege to know. I went to places I had to learn how to pronounce, like Lukachukai (Luke-ah-chew-kai) and Chinle (Chen-ley). I learned about a culture and way of life that was different from any I had known. This however, was not always a solo trek. Many trips to the Navajo Reservation included the company of my daughter Melinda, my sister Beth, and my mother. This collective investigation expanded and enriched myself and my family in ways I can hardly comprehend.

If anyone had told me that at the age of thirty-eight, I would explore a story about Native Americans, World War II, the Marines, and the South Pacific campaigns, I would have reserved a nicely padded room with a view in the nearest mental hospital for them. I had no writing experience to speak of except for a small portfolio of unpublished poems written over my lifetime, and I certainly had no ambition or intention of becoming a published author.

How I arrived at this marvelous journey was a wild ride filled with frustration, exhilaration, amazement, and a belief that there are no coincidences

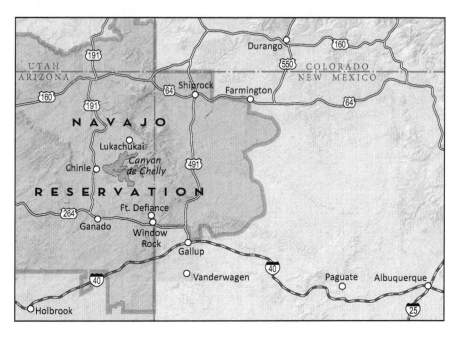

Four Corners area of Arizona, New Mexico, Utah, Colorado, and the Navajo Reservation.

anywhere in the Milky Way Galaxy. I questioned my sanity more times than I can remember and wondered how in the world did I find myself in the position of trying to put together a story that had been classified as "Secret" from 1942 to 1969. I didn't even know where to start, much less end up with a completed manuscript that made sense and accurately portrayed the code talkers' unique service within the Marine Corps. I would have to extract information from a group of veterans who were sworn to secrecy. Not to mention that I was not Navajo and I would be asking these code talkers to reveal things they had never revealed to anyone before.

As you will learn, it was not an easy task, but it was worth pursuing because the code talkers' story is so fascinating and filled with so many honorable human beings. It was worth everything I endured to bring it to fruition. This unfolding journey will also allow me to incorporate more personal stories that are not included in *Navajo Weapon*. So, fasten your seat belts, microwave the popcorn, and enjoy the ride.

CHAPTER 1

AN INTERESTING LITTLE STORY

IN 1988 I WAS LIVING IN BOULDER, COLORADO, as a single parent, working forty hours a week, paying my bills, spending most of my free time trying to keep my daughter occupied with healthy activities, and fairly content with my life. I had good friends, great relationships with my mother and siblings, was a huge fan of the Denver Broncos, and occasionally went out on Friday nights and danced until my feet felt like they would fall off. As hobbies, I crocheted afghan blankets, sewed play clothes for Melinda, and took the usual vacations to Disneyland and Sea World. Little did I know that by August of that year, my life would take a path that was as wonderful as it was strange, and I would never be the same person I had been.

I received a letter from my biological father who was currently residing in Las Vegas. We had been estranged for more than eighteen years (his choice not mine), so his missive was a surprise. He included an article about Navajos that served in the Marine Corps during World War II, and on a Post-it note he wrote, "Isn't this an interesting little story?" They were being honored in Phoenix, Arizona, and the Las Vegas paper picked up the wire story. The article really did not reveal much of what their service entailed and I set aside the article with hardly a second thought. I had no clue why he sent it to me, or more importantly, why he thought I would find it interesting.

A couple of weeks later, I woke up with thoughts of Navajo Marines whirling in my not-yet-awake mind. I was born in 1950, a child of a Navy veteran of World War II, and in school we were taught a great deal about that conflagration. Eleven years past the conclusion, it was still a fresh wound, and I became fairly well informed of what transpired in Europe and the South Pacific. But, I didn't recall learning anything about any Native Americans that served during the war and I was certain that whoever the Navajo code talkers were, I wanted to know more about them.

A question formed in my mind, *What exactly did they do during the war?* I have always been intensely curious by nature, puzzling about things that most people wouldn't give a second thought about. Once this question cemented itself in my mind, I just wanted to find the answer, be satisfied I had it, and move on with my life. So, the first logical place to start was the local library and I checked out the first of many books about the South Pacific conflict. I didn't think that I would have to search very long to find the answer, but I couldn't have been more mistaken. Over the course of the next two months, I devoured over one hundred and thirty books about the South Pacific campaigns and found one small paragraph that briefly mentioned them.

I was stunned! Then I got angry. I have always considered myself a student of American and world history, and much of it I discovered almost always either neglects to mention or passes over indigenous people and their contribution and value to the lands they occupied. I thought to myself, *Is this another example that what Native Americans contribute to this country goes unnoticed? Is it so easy to dismiss them because a majority of Americans do not live next door to their reservations?*

In neighborhoods in most large cities, there are areas with a mixture of cultures: Asian, Jewish, Polish, German, Irish, Italian, etc. Children from these unique neighborhoods mix with each other within the local school system and they have the opportunity to make friends with each other and learn certain aspects of each other's cultures. It can be a true melting pot atmosphere that either fosters understanding and knowledge or bigotry and fear.

The only Native Americans I knew about were the ones portrayed in Hollywood movies, almost exclusively by non-Native American actors. In the movies, a proud, bare-chested warrior, covered in war paint, would wear a feathered war bonnet. He would stride across the plains on a beautiful horse, and was almost always portrayed as a savage, blood-lusting after white people with no shred of civilized behavior. No matter what the circumstances in the movie, it was always justifiable to defeat and kill him. In the back of my mind, I knew there was something definitely wrong with this image, but could never quite put my finger on why I felt that way. I eventually reasoned that it was the result of my biased knowledge of Native Americans that came from history courses and books written from mostly a non-Native American perspective. Tainted history has never sat well with me, and I was determined to find out the reason why the Navajo code talkers had been excluded from the history of one of this country's most important, historical, military conflicts.

The library resources had failed to answer my question, so I decided to go to the next most logical source: the Marine Corps. I formulated a letter under the Freedom of Information Act, requesting any and all information related to the Navajo code talkers of World War II. I sent the letter off and went on with the daily routine of my life.

About six weeks later, an oversized brown envelope arrived in my mailbox and I noticed it was from the Marine Corps Historical Center located in the Washington, D.C. Navy Yard. I quickly got Melinda a snack and set her to her homework before opening the treasure. It was hard to contain the excitement I was feeling. Here, at last, would be the answer to my question. I carefully opened the envelope and withdrew a packet of about thirty-two pages. The top page was a letter stating that my request had produced the enclosed information and if I needed further assistance, to please contact Benis Frank at the Historical Center.

The first three pages were actual military documents, statements from field commanders describing the Navajo code talkers "as general duty Marines they have no peers," and "the Navajos are tractable, easy to command, and perform any duty requested of them without complaint." That struck me as very impressive statements to make about *any* group of Marines. I had spent almost three solid months reading anything and everything about the Marine Corps and I knew they rarely praised any individual or group. The other documents held the same content and tone but didn't explain why the code talkers had no peers, or what type of duty they performed so well.

The rest of the contents were copies of old clippings from various newspapers from the 1970s that resembled the one my father sent me. At the end I knew little more than when I had started. Talk about frustration! Was the Universe playing some twisted joke on me? All I wanted was an answer to my question: *What did they do during the war?* I was really disappointed in the response I received from the one source I believed should have had all the answers. But, I wasn't going to take this without another attempt. I placed a call to the Historical Center and asked where the rest of the documentation on the code talkers was. They replied, "We sent you everything there is to know about the code talkers." I was almost speechless. I couldn't understand how an organization as old and respected as the Marine Corps would have so little information or interest in a group of these unique members.

Now I was determined to find that answer, and concentrated on what my next step should be. Then, it dawned on me. These men were veterans, surely someone within the Veterans Administration (VA) would know how to contact one or more of them. *Genius!* I called the Denver branch of the VA and posed my request. The man I spoke with gave me the name and contact phone number of the Vice President of the Navajo Code Talkers Association in Gallup, New Mexico. I was thrilled! Not only did they have an association, I would gain access to a real live code talker who could answer my question. There is nothing better than hearing the truth directly from the source.

The vice president's name was Harold Foster, and I called him the next day. I didn't realize until much later that we spoke on December 7, the start of one of many goose-bump-inducing events to come. We spoke for about forty-five minutes and after I ended the call, Melinda asked me to whom I was talking. I told her I had just spoken with a Navajo who served during World War II, and then she asked me, "What did he do during the war?"

I looked at her for a moment, then realized I had spent all that time with him, yet I hadn't learned a bloody thing except he was a Marine who served in the 2nd and 5th Marine Divisions! I racked my brain pulling out everything I remembered asking him and realized he'd dodged the very direct question of what he did during the war as effectively as an Olympic fencer. I really didn't quite know what to think, I was puzzled, annoyed, irritated, and mystified that I still had no answer to my question. I thought about calling him right back and trying to engage him in a manner that would satisfy my curiosity, and I'm not sure why I didn't. I guess I was just too frustrated and figured it might be a question for which I would never have a satisfactory answer. Perhaps I simply wasn't entitled to have it.

The Christmas holiday was not far off, so I marshaled my attention and focus on my favorite time of year. Thanksgiving had been a wonderful gathering of family and preparing for Christmas Day always wrapped me in a cocoon of happiness, so I put the thought of the code talkers far back in the recesses of my mind. It would stay there until a couple of months later, when a Navajo appeared at my door and started the quest for the answer in earnest.

CHAPTER 2

HAROLD FOSTER

ONE FRIDAY AFTERNOON IN MID-FEBRUARY, a knock on my door changed my life forever. I opened it to find a woman, mid-forties, who I guessed to be either Hispanic or Native American, asking me if I was Sally McClain. I replied that I was, and she told me her father had instructed her to find me and give me a message.

My first question was, "Who is your father?"

She replied, "Harold Foster." I was so taken aback you could have knocked me over with a dust bunny!

I invited her in, but she declined, so I stepped out onto the porch and asked her who *she* was. She reiterated she was Harold's daughter, she taught elementary school in Arvada and she was surprised how easy it was to find me. Frankly, so was I. Then, without further conversation, she told me to please call Harold tomorrow morning around 6:00 am. She turned and walked off the porch, out to her car, and was gone before I had the presence of mind to ask her name or thank her for the message.

It had been about two and a half months since our first contact, and I had no idea what prompted Mr. Foster to seek me out at this time. My curiosity was definitely piqued and I quickly searched though a stack of papers on my kitchen table hoping and praying I still had his phone number. Relieved that I still had it, I made a quick note reminding myself to set my alarm for 5:45 am Saturday morning and put it on my clock in my bedroom. I spent the rest of the day cleaning the house, doing dishes, and trying not to think what tomorrow morning's conversation might possibly reveal.

My dreams that night were a jumbled mass of visions, where black sand was deeply splotched in blood, figures of humans lying in crooked, almost marionette-like positions, faces with no eyes, voices talking in a garbled language whipping through radio sets, and far off in the background, a deep, throbbing, primal drum beat mingled with singing I didn't recognize. When the alarm went off, I came out of my sleep startled, looking around and saying one word, *"Iwo."* I peeled back the covers, half expecting to see myself covered in gritty, coarse, black volcanic sand. That dream had been so real, so visceral, that I could still detect a very faint smell of sulfur. I jumped out of bed, ran to the kitchen, turned on the light, and immediately started smelling around the stove for a possible gas leak. Realizing one didn't exist, I put the teakettle on for a cup of my one and only coffee preference: Swiss Mocha. I glanced at the clock and assured myself that I had not missed the appointed time to call Mr. Foster. The coffee should be ready at the precise moment to dial his number.

The phone rang and was picked up after the first ring. "Hello. May I speak with Harold Foster?" I stated.

"This is Harold. Did my daughter have any trouble finding you?" he asked.

"No, but I was very surprised that you sent her to find me," I said. There was a rather long pause and for a moment I thought he changed his mind and hung up on me.

"Mr. Foster?" I said.

"I'm still here, I was waiting for you to ask me a question," he replied.

"Oh, I was just wondering why you wanted me to call you." I said.

Another long pause and then he answered, "You need to come to Navajo land if you want your questions answered. I don't tell people about the war over the phone, I need to see you face to face."

I was startled. Why was he so reluctant to answer my question over the phone? But I was so intrigued, that I told him I would be able to arrange a trip to the Navajo Reservation around the second week of April. He replied, "This is my address, write to me and we will arrange a good time to meet in Window Rock." I wrote down his postal address and thanked him for his time before realizing he had hung up the phone after he completed giving me the address. I wasn't sure if I should be shocked or offended by his seeming rudeness. I reminded myself that I was dealing with a people and culture of which I was woefully ignorant, and shouldn't rush to any judgments.

I settled at the kitchen table, sipping and savoring my coffee watching a beautiful sunrise and trying to shake the dark images left from the night before. Then I glanced at the calendar and felt a cold chill all over my body. The date was February 19th. Why was that date ringing a bell? It came to me in a flood of remembering … February 19, 1945 was debarkation day for Iwo Jima. I was beginning to think there were forces at work I couldn't comprehend, first the call with Harold on December 7 and now one on February 19. All of that could have been called a coincidence, but the dream that preceded the call on the 19 made me a little uneasy. Another dream six years later would bring clarity to many unanswered questions.

Throughout my life, my dreams have always been very vivid, full of sights and sounds and occasionally prescient. I have had dreams that came to fruition within a matter of days of their occurrences. As Melinda stirred from her bedroom, I decided to plan a trip to Arizona and finally resolve once and for all the question of what the code talkers did during the war.

APRIL

From the second phone call to my departure date was just about two months and during that time, Harold and I had exchanged a few letters and a handful of phone calls. The contents were really quite ordinary: background information on where I grew up and my family, and on where he grew up and his family. I hoped that I was building a small bridge of trust that would allow Harold to feel comfortable enough to answer my question. I arranged time off from work and Melinda was going to stay with my sister Dona and my mother. I mapped out my route from Boulder to Gallup, New Mexico. I packed a bag, made a motel reservation, and planned to depart around 5:00 am Thursday morning, to return on Monday. It would be a ten-hour drive and I was excited to be in a part of the country I had never visited. I made sure my car had an oil change, full tank of gas, and plenty of cassettes of my favorite music.

The road from Albuquerque to Gallup went through some of the most starkly beautiful land I had ever seen. Off in the distance were sandstone formations bleached to a chalk white dotted with small sections of mesquite and pine trees. The closer I got to Gallup, I began to feel an energy; ancient and somewhat foreign to my own experiences. Then I saw the sign—Route 66—and memories flooded through me as I recalled scenes from the 1960s

Harold Foster, Fort Defiance, Arizona, 1989.

television show, *Route 66*. As I drove down this historic highway that ran through the heart of Gallup, I saw my first glimpse of what a Navajo looked like. I also noted the many stores that advertised Navajo goods and something called "dead pawn." I had no idea what that meant and wasn't sure I wanted to know. I finally arrived at the motel, checked in, unloaded the car, cleaned out the trash from the meals and drinks I'd consumed during the long drive, and immediately took a shower.

I had arranged to contact Harold the next morning, and we would meet Saturday somewhere in Window Rock, Arizona, which was only about an hour and a half north and slightly west of Gallup. Feeling refreshed, I got back in my car and headed toward the center of Gallup to do some window shopping. I went into one of the shops and was mesmerized by the incredible beauty of Navajo jewelry, rugs, and sandpaintings. I eventually worked up the nerve to ask a clerk what "dead pawn" was. He explained that it was any possession that had been pawned, and if not claimed within ninety days, the shop owner was allowed to sell it.

I tried to imagine what desperate circumstances would force anyone to pawn such beautiful property, and realized poverty must be deep within the Navajo community for this to take place on a regular basis. I found a beautiful disposable lighter cover for my sister Beth and delicate silver and turquoise bracelets for Melinda, Dona, and Mom. My growling stomach put an end to my shopping spree, and I asked a clerk where was a good place to eat and she recommended the Ranch Kitchen. It was located just about a half-mile from my hotel, so I set out for it.

I returned to the hotel after a delicious dinner and fell asleep watching television. I woke around two in the morning, turned off the television, and went back to sleep. I spent all day Friday walking around Gallup, visiting art galleries, and marveling at the artistic wares that the Navajos, Hopis and Zunis created and sold. I was fascinated with the kachina figures the Hopis made and asked about the history of several of them. I also noticed many items by R. C. Gorman and realized the family connection; R. C. was Carl Gorman's son. I knew about Carl Gorman and his artwork and realized the apple didn't fall far from that tree. That entire day I tried to absorb as much information about Navajo art and culture as possible. I began to feel that I was gaining an understanding of the people, and knew this might help me during my meeting with Harold.

The next morning the alarm went off at 8:00 am and I placed a call to Harold. He asked me how my trip was and said he was looking forward to meeting with me for lunch. I got the distinct impression he was not going to answer any questions until we were face to face, so I asked him about the history of Gallup. He said, "It was originally a part of Navajo land until 1868, then it was relinquished as part of a treaty the tribe signed with the United States. Nowadays, however it's considered a "border" town, with a not so nice reputation in the treatment of the Navajos."

He quickly changed the subject and asked me how I found the surrounding area and I replied that I thought this part of the country was beautiful. For the first time since I started the search for the answer to the question, *"What did they do during the war?,"* I felt that I was finally going to achieve that end. I had no idea how misguided I was.

WINDOW ROCK

Window Rock is the current tribal capital of the Navajo Nation and is located in Arizona just across the border from New Mexico. After I spoke with Harold and agreed to meet him for lunch at the Navajo Nation Inn, I took out my road atlas and plotted my route. If I thought the sandstone formations from Albuquerque to Gallup were incredible, the sienna-colored formations along the highway to Window Rock were breathtakingly beautiful. They looked as if a giant artist's hand had sculpted and painted each and every one of them.

Ribbons of different colored bands flowed in horizontal patterns that almost made me forget to breathe. I pulled over at one spot and took out my camera and took over a dozen different shots, seeing them alter almost as if by magic as the rising sun changed the colors from dusty to light. Off in the distance I heard the sound of bleating sheep and noticed a sign on the side of the road advertising "fat sheep for sale." I had to laugh. Would anyone want to buy a "skinny" sheep and was there any difference? I guessed that a "fat" sheep was one that had not been sheared yet.

I resumed my course to Window Rock and saw that the Navajo Nation Inn was located right on the highway. I pulled into the huge parking area, then headed for the entrance. I arrived about ten minutes before the appointed time and decided to use those few minutes observing the pictures I noticed on the walls that showed the names and dates of past and present Navajo Tribal Presidents. I then approached a lovely young Navajo woman stationed at the counter and asked if Mr. Foster had arrived yet. She looked at me with wary eyes, grabbed a menu, and said to follow her. I entered the dining area and she led me to a booth where

Harold Foster was sitting. He rose, and I introduced myself. He was wearing a western-style shirt and a bolo tie, and on his left wrist was a beautiful handmade leather cuff that was surrounded by large pieces of turquoise with a timepiece in the middle. His face was deep brown and he had very pleasant-looking eyes. I felt that I was, at last going to have the answer to my question.

As I sat down, I felt every eye in that room on me. It startled me to be stared at. I wondered if I was dressed inappropriately. I was wearing nice slacks and a blue short-sleeve cotton top, neither of which was too tight or too revealing. The only make-up I had on was a little mascara, blush, and lip gloss, my hair was clean and styled, and I had worn no jewelry. I decided that I would not freak out about how I was being examined by the twenty-plus Navajos in the dining room.

Harold asked me how my drive had been, and we spent about ten minutes in general conversation. I was very unsure of how to go about getting my question answered without appearing to be overly nosy, so I asked him how he came to join the Marine Corps.

He smiled and said his brother Daniel had joined in early 1942, and when he came home on leave he told me "the Marines was a good organization and I should think about joining when I reached seventeen. Jobs on the reservation were really hard to get and the war had made it even more difficult. Daniel said he might make the Marine Corps his career.

"I was impressed with how different my brother walked and talked. He had a confidence I had never seen before and I was very impressed. As my older brother, he had always been someone I looked up to, but when he showed up at home in that uniform, I knew I wanted to look and act just like he did. When two Navajo recruiters, Johnny Manuelito and John Benally, showed up at our school and told us about the Marine Corps, how we would get to travel and see places far from America and serve in the best military organization in the world, I couldn't wait to join up. I joined after I turned seventeen and after boot camp was assigned to the 2nd Marine Division. My first action was on Tarawa."

"Tarawa? That was a really intense and difficult battle. What was your job?" I asked.

He frowned and said in a very flat tone, "I was a radioman and helped coordinate the movement of the Marines once they hit the beaches. Tarawa was a bad place, so many Marines died because there was no cover on the beaches and the Japanese fire was intense and constant."

I could sense that my asking him to reveal any more of that battle would be extremely uncomfortable for him. I was really unsure if I should ask him anything else. I certainly didn't want to have him clam up before I got the answer to my question. So, I changed the subject back to boot camp. "Did you find boot camp a difficult experience?" I asked.

He smiled and said, "Boot camp was not so hard for us Navajos. We were marched to meals, classes, and to church in the government boarding schools, so we already knew some types of strict discipline. Obeying an order without question is something we learn from our grandmothers when we are very young. In fact, my grandmother would have made a good drill instructor." He laughed and so did I. I couldn't imagine any grandmother being as good a drill instructor as a seasoned Marine and I found the comparison rather odd. I would later learn just how true Harold's statement had been.

I finally had to ask why everyone in the dining room was staring at us so I turned to him and said, "Have I done something wrong? Everyone is staring at us."

Harold looked around the room and in a very lighthearted tone replied, "They're not used to seeing a white face out of tourist season." I didn't know how to react to that statement. Was he teasing me? Was he humoring me? I found out later the reason I was under suspicion was that the Navajo people had become very aware of the code talkers over the last eighteen years, and were not only extremely proud of them, but very protective too. Seeing a revered, respected elder with a strange white person was, in their minds, a cause for concern.

Then, something amazing happened. I felt this man enter the room before I actually saw him. He was wearing a bright red jacket, red T-shirt, and dark colored slacks. His white hair was pulled back into an unusual-looking configuration at the back of his head called a *chondo*, and he was walking with a cane. *Carl Gorman!* I could hardly believe whom I was seeing. I knew of him from his artistic reputation, and his son R. C. was equally as famous. I turned to Harold and asked, "Is that Carl Gorman?"

Harold's face was suddenly a mask as he replied, "Yeah, that's Carl." I didn't quite understand this sudden coolness in his voice. Were they enemies? If they were, I certainly wasn't going to broach the subject. I felt I was so close to learning the truth of the type of service they rendered during the war, I wasn't about to say anything that would ruin that chance. So, Harold picked up where he left off by telling me that after the battle on Tarawa, he was transferred to the 5th Marine Division.

"You were on Iwo Jima?" I said. He nodded his head and before I could ask him anything more, Carl suddenly appeared at our booth. I was awestruck. This man had a presence about him that was tangible, and I definitely wanted to speak with him.

He abruptly said, "Who are you?" I held out my hand, he took it, and I said, "I'm Sally McClain." He spoke in Navajo to Harold and then sat down to my right in the booth. I felt a little giddy being next to him—he was an incredible artist and I sensed a very special human being.

"What are you doing here with Mr. Foster?" he asked. I told him I was trying to find out what he did during the war. He spoke to Harold again in Navajo and the tone of their exchange sounded clipped and a little sharp. I had never heard a Native American language and Navajo had a lyrical quality to it that fascinated me. It didn't even bother me that they were probably talking about me—I was just hoping to get my question answered.

Then Carl said something that floored me, "I served in the 2nd Marine Division and used Navajo to talk the Japanese to death." I was momentarily speechless! I didn't quite know what to say and he looked at me as if he was waiting for me to ask him more.

I gathered my thoughts and said, "When did you join the Marine Corps?"

"1942," he replied. Then he asked me where I was from and I told him Boulder, Colorado. Then again, he asked me why I was asking Mr. Foster questions about what he did during the war.

I told him an abbreviated version of my search for what the code talkers did during the war and said, "I just want to know exactly what service the code talkers rendered during the war."

He folded his hands on the table, spoke to Harold again and then said, "Well, Harold and I have agreed to tell you what you want to know, but then we're going to have to kill you."

What? I was startled, to say the least, then I noticed a slight twinkle in both their eyes. *Oh, you're testing me or you're playing with me, but either way I get it. I grew up with four brothers who taught me how to stand up for myself and have never been the kind of person you can bully, threaten, or intimidate. Bring it!*

I looked first at Harold, then Carl, and stated with a coy smile, "Well gentlemen, I'll take you up on that offer because I know that I can outrun both of you and anyone else in this room!" They both roared with laughter and I knew

I was going to get what I came for. Carl asked me how long I was staying and I said only until Monday. Lunch was clearly over and all three of us walked out to the parking lot. This is where I received a major shock. Carl's red SUV was covered from front to back in all manner of Marine Corps decals and stickers. I finally noticed that the red jacket he was wearing had a huge Marine Corps logo silk-screened on the back.

I looked from Carl to his car several times and had a difficult time reconciling this renowned, sensitive artist with the image of a Marine. For lack of a better phrase, it simply did not compute. Carl took a business card from his wallet, handed it to me and said, "You have to call my wife Mary." I didn't know *why* I had to speak with his wife, but he became very agitated and repeated again, "you have to call my wife, you're the one, you have to call my wife, you're the one." I didn't know why he kept saying I was "the one" but to calm him down I promised to call her after I got home.

He got into his car, peeled out of the parking lot like a bat out of hell, and roared down the highway. I asked Harold, "Does he always drive like that? Isn't he afraid of getting a ticket?"

Harold laughed and said, "There isn't a reservation cop anywhere who would dare give the old man a ticket for anything."

I turned and thanked Harold for meeting with me and he asked if he could see me tomorrow. "I would appreciate you giving me more time to fully answer my questions. Where do you want to meet and what time?" I replied. He said he would come down to Gallup and meet with me in my motel room and would bring some material for me to look at. I thanked him, bade him a good afternoon, and headed back to Gallup.

This was the strangest and most fascinating day I'd had in a long time. Questions swirled through my mind, and I went over everything I had been told. I realized I still knew very little of what they actually did, and Carl said he "talked the Japanese to death." I couldn't imagine how that was accomplished, but perhaps what Harold was bringing me tomorrow would answer that.

Harold arrived at my motel at ten o'clock, and as we sat at a little table, he gave me a yellow booklet. It was a program from the Navajo Code Talkers Association Awards Ceremony Banquet held in 1986. It contained a chronology of the code talkers and the events in the South Pacific Theatre. There were wonderful black and white combat photographs along with ones showing association members marching in the Tournament of Roses and the Gallup Inter-tribal Indian Ceremonial parade. It looked like a wonderful source of information and I was anxious to read it through.

"You can have this copy," Harold said.

"Thank you, this sounds like a wonderful program, you must be very proud to be a member of this association," I replied.

He nodded his head in agreement and a rather uncomfortable silence ensued. I wasn't sure whether I should wait it out or ask some questions. Harold broke the silence when he said, "Carl claims to be one of 'The First 29' but I don't believe him."

"What are The First 29? " I asked.

Harold looked out the window and then said, "The First 29 say they were the Navajos who built the first code, but no one ever said anything about them when I was in the code school. The white instructor, Philip Johnston, always said it was his idea, so I think Carl's full of it."

Wow. His tone was tinged with just a hint of disgust and perhaps a touch of jealousy. I really didn't know how to respond, so I asked him about Philip Johnston. Harold replied, "Johnston was an instructor at the school and said he grew up around Leuppe. His father was a missionary on the rez and he said he brought the idea of radiomen talking Navajo to the big shots of the Marine Corps. That's how it all started and the Marines liked it so much they started recruiting Navajos for this duty. What time do you leave tomorrow?"

This quick change of subject indicated to me that the question and answer session was definitely over. "I'll leave around five, because it is a ten-hour drive back to Boulder," I replied. He stood up, shook my hand, and told me to have a safe trip back, then left my room. Now I was really puzzled. I picked up the program he gave me and started reading it. When I was done, I had no more of a clue as to what the code talkers actually did during the war than I had had the previous day. But it listed the names of deceased code talkers and ones that were killed in battle. This was starting to irritate the hell out of me. All I wanted was an answer to my question, yet the harder I tried to find, it the more elusive it became. I was not accustomed to seeking something and not finding the answer, and it just made me all the more determined to find it. Perhaps Carl's wife Mary would be of more help, and I would definitely make a point of calling her once I got home.

The drive back was long and uneventful. I was really looking forward to seeing Melinda and telling her, Mom, and Dona about the trip. Mom and Dona didn't ask too many questions. I suppose they were wondering why I was on this rather strange wild goose chase, and frankly I was beginning to wonder the same thing myself. I wouldn't be in the dark for much longer, because I was determined to have my answer from Mary Gorman and then get on with my life.

CHAPTER 3

CARL AND MARY GORMAN

I HAD BEEN BACK FROM GALLUP just a little over four days when I remembered I was supposed to call Mary Gorman. So, after feeding Melinda, making sure her homework was done, dinner was eaten, and she was tucked into bed, I retrieved Carl's business card and dialed the number.

A woman's voice answered and I asked to speak with Mary Gorman. "This is Mary," she replied.

"My name is Sally McClain and I met your husband last weekend and he asked me to give you a call," I replied.

"Yes," she said and then there was a long pause.

I finally said "Uh, can you tell me anything about what Carl did during the war?"

"Yes," she replied and another long pause ensued. This was getting ridiculous! What was so difficult about this subject that so far everyone I had broached was reluctant as hell to answer my questions?

Perhaps sensing my frustration Mary said, "I understand you were meeting with Harold Foster when you met Carl?"

"Yes," I replied.

"Why do you want to know what they did during the war?" she asked. Finally, an opening! I explained about the article I received about the code talkers, my futile search through the library, and the seemingly incomplete answers from the Marine Corps Historical Center. I just wanted an answer to that question.

"I'm afraid you may have bitten off more than you can chew," she replied.

"Uh, I'm sorry, why is that?" I asked.

"Because", she stated, "there is no simple or easy answer to give you."

"Okay," I said, "is it possible to give me a condensed version?"

"No not really. I think you need to come back down to the reservation and do some more research. If you want your questions answered, you need to know more about the people who became the code talkers," she said. Then it was my turn to pause.

I finally said. "I would really like to do that, but I can't take any more vacation time until the last week in August."

"Well," she answered, "that would be a good time for us and I think you will find the trip worth your while."

"Okay," I replied, "can I write to you at the address on Carl's business card when I have the exact dates?"

"I'll look forward to receiving your letter. Have a nice evening," she replied and hung up the phone.

That was *the* strangest conversation I'd had to date. Why was it necessary for me to know about the code talkers as Navajos in order for me to get the answers I was seeking? As Mary suggested, maybe this was something more than I bargained for. But, my curiosity would simply not be satisfied until I had what I needed. I went back to work and requested vacation time off for the last three days of August. Actually with the Labor Day holiday, I would have almost an entire week to find what I was looking for.

In the meantime, I went back to the library and checked out several books about the Navajo people. I fell in love with the small part of the reservation I had driven through, and it certainly wouldn't hurt to know more about a people and culture of which I was woefully ignorant.

The Navajos are a fascinating people; they grow corn, beans, and a variety of squash, and have large herds of sheep, goats, horses, and cattle. They have lived on their land for over eight thousand years, and have always been non-nomadic in nature. Their language is difficult to write, and everything they know about their heritage is passed orally from parent to child. They have an impressive ability for memorization. I became deeply impressed with the Navajos and looked forward to my next visit to the reservation. The books about the Navajo people were, for the most part well written, but in many ways hard to read.

The United States had dealt a harsh blow to them from 1865 to 1868 and it made me angry that they had been treated so unjustly. The Long Walk, as it became known, was a forced march some 350 miles southwest from their ancestral land to exile in Bosque Redondo in the New Mexico territory. Anglos hoped to find gold on Navajo land and this was the primary reason for their

Carl Gorman, Fort Defiance, Arizona, 1993.

displacement. They suffered unspeakable living conditions and desperate pleas from their Head Men finally created a commission that eventually saved them. The Navajo people signed a treaty in 1868, agreeing to cede some portions of their land to the government if they were allowed to go home. Having found no gold on Navajo land, the government representatives agreed to the terms of a treaty, and the Navajos were allowed to return to their sacred homeland.

I was a little ashamed of myself that there are Native American nations existing in this country that I have little knowledge of or interest in. I was well aware of the American Indian Movement (AIM) that was politically very active during the 70s but I never contemplated their plight or the struggles they face on a daily basis. The old saying, "out of sight, out of mind," was all too true for me. So, I made it my priority to try to absorb as much knowledge about the Navajos as possible.

I learned about *hozhone*, the Navajo belief that everything in life must be balanced; mentally, physically, and spiritually. You always greet the rising sun with a prayer and the promise of maintaining balance throughout the day. If you succeed, great! If you don't, well you get to rise the next morning and try it again. No punishment, no reward, just the satisfaction in the effort. What a wonderful concept. Their clan system prohibits any intermarriage within the clan, and modesty is the rule, not the exception. They are a quiet, humble people who believe that any manner or form of bragging is the worst kind of behavior and is to be avoided. Grandparents, and particularly the grandmothers, are responsible for disciplining and teaching the children. Grandparents are to be obeyed without question, and bad behavior is corrected immediately.

The Navajos have a Star People Clan, who they believe descended from the Holy People, who live somewhere in the universe. They aren't necessarily more powerful or special than the rest of the Navajos, they just come from "elsewhere." I was fascinated to hear about the Star Clan. Navajos believe that the land they live on is a sacred part of Mother Earth. It is to be protected at all cost, and if treated with respect and reverence, it will provide everything they need. They view drought with the same temperament as a plentiful time; in balance. Everything is always in balance.

But I found the most interesting aspect of Navajo culture is that it is matrilineal. The women hold the land and livestock. A man marries into his wife's clan, but everything from the home to the livestock belongs to her. He is responsible for maintaining the home and selling the wool and the livestock, but if they part ways, she keeps everything. Now, that's a concept and way of life I could really appreciate!

Summer was fast approaching and I registered Melinda for a two-week YMCA camp. Being a single parent, I learned the value of time away from one another. She got concentrated time with her friends, swimming, camping, and activities, while I got some real time for myself and I know that it made our relationship a lot easier in so many ways. It was wonderful to come home after a long day at work and not have to cook dinner if I wasn't hungry. Sitting on the couch for a couple of hours with a bowl of popcorn and a book was a real luxury.

The summer raced along and before I knew it, it was time for the trip back to Gallup. I asked my mom if she would like to come with me and Melinda, and she readily agreed. During my childhood, we took many road trips to Oklahoma for family reunions and I always enjoyed these adventures. Melinda was a good traveler, never the "Are we there yet?" type of child, and I knew that she and Mom would get to see a part of the country they had not seen before. I wrote to Mary and told her the dates we would be in Gallup, and asked when we could all meet. She replied a few days later, and said their schedule was wide open, and to call her the moment we arrived, so we could arrange the meeting time and place.

I felt fairly confident that I had done my homework about the Navajo people. During the long drive I related what I had learned to Mom and Melinda. I was anxious to finally have my questions answered, and hoped this would end up being a great experience for all of us. Driving down Route 66, I pointed out some of the businesses I had visited. Over the last few years, Mom had often worked in art galleries in Boulder, so she knew a lot more about Native American art than I did. We checked into the motel, unpacked the car, and then I called Mary and arranged to meet her and Carl for lunch the next day. We headed back to town and enjoyed dinner at the Ranch Kitchen before turning in for the night.

The next morning, we went out for breakfast and did more window-shopping before heading for the Denny's restaurant, where we were meeting the Gormans. As we entered, I noticed Carl right away. He was hard to miss and he was sitting next to a woman who looked about my mother's age, dressed in a calico skirt and blue blouse, and wearing her white hair in the same style as Carl's. *That must be Mary.* Then I realized she was not a Navajo. I tried not to let my surprise show as we walked toward their table.

Carl noticed me and waved, and I introduced Mom, my daughter, and myself, and then we all sat down. The conversation was general and light and the food was excellent. From my previous encounter with Harold, I knew that to ask any questions about what Carl did during the war was simply not a wise thing to pursue. So, I turned and asked Mary where she grew up. "I was born in Rhode Island, but during and after the war my parents and I lived in Los Angeles. That's where I met Carl," she replied.

Then I decided to go out on a limb and asked, "What are The First 29?"

Mary smiled and said, "What did Harold tell you about them?" I repeated to her what Harold said, and she sighed. "It saddens me that there are some code talkers who choose not to believe that The First 29 existed."

"I forgot—who was Philip Johnston?" I asked.

"Supposedly he gave a demonstration to the Marine Corps using the Navajo language in combat for sending coded messages. The Marine Corps liked the

Mary Gorman, Gallup,
New Mexico, ca. 2000.

idea so much, they recruited twenty-nine Navajos for special duty. Carl, along with Eugene Crawford, Wilsie Bitsie and twenty-six other Navajos were sworn into the Marine Corps in April 1942. They were the first all Native American platoon in Marine Corps history. Philip Johnston took public credit for something he had no right to," she replied.

"Why doesn't Harold believe Carl about The First 29?" I asked.

"Well," replied Mary, "some Navajos have a problem with members of the tribe that achieve success outside of the reservation, jealousy I suppose. But the story of The First 29 does sound like an unlikely tale, especially when no proof has been found. Some need to see before they believe. Isn't that why you are here?"

"Uh, no," I replied, "I'm not necessarily the kind of person that needs proof of something before I believe it. I know lots of things I can't explain how or why I believe, I just know what I know. I'm here because I just wanted my question answered."

Mary smiled and said, "As I said before, the answer to your question is not an easy one. Traditionally, when Navajos return from war, they go through purification ceremonies and once they are concluded, they are not to speak about their experiences lest it return and give them nightmares. You are going to have to work very hard to get your answer. The Navajos who served as code talkers are very proud of what they did, but they'll be extremely reluctant to talk about it. But, it is a story that deserves and needs to be told, so if you are willing and patient, the answer you seek will be revealed. Are you willing to do that?"

I wasn't sure how to answer that question. Did I really have to know this answer? *No! Uh, yes!* This puzzle was too intriguing for me to leave unsolved. I just wasn't sure how much work it would take to achieve it. "Well," I replied, "I do want to know the answer I'm just not sure how to go about getting it. Do you have any advice for me?"

"We'll talk about that at another time," she replied. *Oh goody, I get to wait until another time to get an answer!* This was almost getting to be a little too mysterious for me. But, I didn't have many options at this point, so I decided to slow down and take it as it came.

Lunch concluded and Mary asked me to call her in the evening, because she knew some code talkers who might be willing to meet with me. I asked if Carl would be willing to answer some questions and Mary said, "Carl already talked about his war experiences in his autobiography and it's doubtful he would ever talk about it again. He might, but don't count on it." I was really disappointed. I liked being around Carl and Mary and wanted to spend a lot more time with them, but if he couldn't or wouldn't talk about his experiences there was nothing I could do about it. I had to hope that perhaps the code talkers to whom Mary would refer me would not have any objections to my questions. Mom, Melinda, and I drove back to the motel. The two of them laid down for a nap while I drove back into Gallup to visit the town museum.

After dinner, I called Mary and she said Carl had arranged for me to meet with four code talkers the next day at the Gallup Chamber of Commerce at 2:00 p.m. The only advice she gave me was to let the men talk, say what they felt comfortable revealing, and don't interrupt them with questions. She wished me luck and said to call her after the meeting ended. I was really happy! I just might be able to *finally* get the answer I had been seeking. I told Mom and Melinda about the meeting and suggested they drop me off while they drove to Sky City. Sky City, fifty minutes east of Gallup, New Mexico, is a place where in the past the tribe of Acoma Pueblo constructed their city 367 feet high on a plateau of a sheer vertical sandstone formation in order to be safe from their enemies. Beginning in A.D. 1150, it is the oldest continually inhabited community in North America. It sounded fascinating and I was glad Melinda was going to share that experience with her grandmother.

THE DISCUSSION

The next day, Mom dropped me off at the Chamber of Commerce and I eagerly awaited the arrival of the code talkers. I was shown into the main meeting room and sat down at a long table. I was alone only a few moments then four Navajos entered and walked toward me. I stood up, held out my hand and we introduced ourselves. John Kinsel, Tom Begay, Bill Toledo, and Dean Wilson sat down around the table. I thanked them for meeting with me and stated I wanted to know what they had done during the war.

There was a brief silence before Dean Wilson spoke. "I was only sixteen when the Marine Corps recruiter came to the reservation and tried to sign us up to join. When the recruiter took a break, I noticed he set aside my application in a pile that was for men too young to join. I would have turned seventeen in

November and I wanted to join now, so I pulled my papers out and put them in the pile where Carl Gorman and Eugene Crawford's papers were. That's how I got into the Corps. I served in the 2nd Marine Division and after the war became a tribal judge."

After a respectable pause, John Kinsel spoke next. "I was in my final year of school when Johnny Manuelito and John Benally came to talk with us. They looked so sharp in their uniforms, they walked straight and tall, and they said the Marines were 'the first to fight' and 'only the best man became a Marine.' I was sold! I loved the poster of the Marine in his dress blues. That uniform really spoke to me and I swore I wanted one just like it. I was a member of an all-Navajo platoon and was assigned to the 3rd Marine Division. I was on Bougainville, Guam, and Iwo Jima. On Iwo, I was wounded and evacuated about half way through the battle. That was a bad place."

Tom Begay spoke next. "In boot camp, they teach you how to march, drill, shoot, everything you need to survive during combat. In the mess hall, you're told to eat everything put on your plate. The food was really good, so it wasn't a problem until it came to the funny yellow stuff. On my first day, I ate all my breakfast and walked toward the end of the hall where you leave your tray when a sergeant stopped me. He told me my plate wasn't clean and it better be before I left. I looked at the funny yellow stuff because it was the only thing left on the plate, scooped it up, and swallowed it whole."

At this, all of the men were smiling and laughing at this remembrance. "I assume that the funny yellow stuff was butter?" I asked.

Tom nodded his head and then continued. "I didn't know what butter was, never had it growing up or in the boarding school meals. It tasted like grease and I never got used to that, but I ate it because that sergeant said I had to and you obeyed your elders! I was raised in the Navajo traditions, carried a small pouch of corn pollen around my neck. I used it in my morning prayers. Boot camp was strict and hard, but you were grateful for all that training when you were in combat."

Heads nodded in agreement all around. Then Bill Toledo spoke. "I was in the same platoon with Mr. Kinsel and my cousin Preston Toledo, and served in the 3rd Marine Division, Headquarters and Service section. After the war, I didn't tell anyone what I did. A couple of years ago, my wife and daughter were cleaning the house and my military picture fell off the mantle and the glass broke. My daughter cleaned it up, but she noticed that some papers were stuffed behind it. She unfolded them and called my wife and me into the room. 'Mom, did you know we have a famous code talker in the family?' That's how my family found out, and I told them some things about the war."

All of this was absolutely fascinating. These men were probably telling me things they had never divulged before and I felt very humble. However, they still had not really told me exactly what they did during the war. I remembered Mary's warning and resisted the urge to start asking questions.

The long silence was finally broken when Dean Wilson crossed his arms across his chest and glowered at me. *Oh, crap! Did I do something wrong? Mr. Wilson does not look pleased.* I had no idea that what was about to happen would change my life forever. All of a sudden, he broke the silence and unloaded on me.

"DON'T YOU KNOW WE'RE OLD!? DON'T YOU KNOW WE'RE GOING TO DIE AND NOBODY WILL KNOW WHAT WE DID!? WHY AREN'T YOU WRITING THIS DOWN!?"

I was startled ... stunned! I certainly didn't expect that reaction! Why on earth would I need to write down what they were telling me? To avoid a further dressing down, I frantically looked around for something to write on and at that moment I would have sold my only child for a piece of paper. Bill Toledo saved me by tearing off a sheet from a tablet he had with him and handed it to me.

I immediately apologized for not taking notes and hoped I had not offended them. Dean uncrossed his arms and asked, "Do we need to repeat what we told you?"

"No," I replied, "I have a good memory and think I've got everything you talked about. Mr. Wilson, were you one of The First 29? "

Dean nodded his head and then said, "That was the hardest thing I ever had to do. Trying to find words for military terms that we could use in messages, well, it gave all of us headaches! You need to talk to Eugene Crawford and Wilsie Bitsie, they'll tell you more about that time. They served in the Raider Battalions."

"Thank you for that information, I'll definitely try to speak with them," I said. Then, as if by some secret, unspoken message, they all stood up and left the room. I sat there for I don't know how long writing down everything the men had said, before someone came into the room and said they needed to close up for the day. Nearly four hours had passed in the blink of an eye, and I was still uncertain as to what just exactly had happened. I stepped out onto the street just as Mom drove up.

We drove in silence back to the hotel. Melinda finally broke it when she related what she had seen that day and how sad the story was of the grandmother and child that jumped from the top of the plateau city to avoid capture by the Spaniards. I nodded in sympathy, but my ears were really not registering what she was saying. I needed to get to a phone and ask Mary some direct questions, and this time she was not going to dance away from giving me straight answers!

As soon as we returned to the motel room, I called Mary and asked if I could meet with her and Carl as soon as possible. She told me they could meet with me around eight, and gave me directions to their house in Fort Defiance. The three of us went out to dinner, and I asked mom if it would be okay for her to stay with Melinda while I went to the Gormans' house. Mom was a little tired after the emotional day at Sky City and was happy to stay in and watch television with Melinda.

I set out for Fort Defiance with a resolve to have my question answered once and for all. I would accept nothing less and that was all there was to it. Ever heard, "Be careful what you wish for?"

CHAPTER 4

"THE ONE"

I ARRIVED AT THE GORMANS' HOUSE A FEW MINUTES BEFORE EIGHT O'CLOCK. The sun was just setting and the sky was streaked with ribbons of pink- and orange-tinted clouds. I gathered myself and knocked on the door. Mary opened it and asked me in.

The front room walls were covered with Carl's paintings, many of which I recognized, and the kitchen table was covered in piles of papers. Carl was sitting at the head, absorbed in what looked like other people's artwork. Mary explained that Carl was teaching an art course at the University of New Mexico, Gallup campus. He looked up, smiled at me, and then went back to his work. Mary asked me if I would like a glass of tea and I replied, "Yes, thank you."

I was momentarily distracted looking around the two rooms, because for me, admiring Carl's work was a real treat. His horse paintings were striking, simple in their composition and yet very powerful. Mary interrupted my reverie and asked me to sit down in the living room.

"How did your meeting go today?" she asked. I related what had happened, how in the end Dean had scolded me for not writing down what I was being told. The whole time, Mary was smiling and fighting back the urge to laugh. Frankly, by this time I found little that was amusing about any of this.

She sensed my mood and said, "Did you get the answer you were seeking?"

"No," I said, "I didn't. It was nice that they were telling me about some of their experiences, but it was clear to me they weren't going to stay and answer any questions."

"Well," Mary said, "I can give you some of the details if that's what you want, but it may create more questions than answers. Will you be satisfied with the simple explanation I can give you?"

YES! Uh... NO! I came here to get my answer, Mary is willing to give it to me, so why should there be any hesitation?

Finally I said, "Why do I get the feeling that this is some kind of trick or test?"

Carl and Mary looked at each other for a moment then he replied, "Because if all you came for was a simple answer you can have it, but if you want the whole truth, that's not going to be simple. So which do you want?"

Crap! Now what? Do I just want an answer or do I want the whole truth? Is there a difference?

"Before you answer," Carl said, "remember when I said, 'you're the one'?" I nodded my head in agreement. "Why do you think I said that?"

I stared at him, I had no clue why he said that to me, but do I confess that now? "I, well … no I don't know why you said that to me. Can you explain it?" I said.

Mary spoke, and I'll never forget this conversation as long as I live. "When Carl met you and saw you were meeting with Harold, asking what he did during the war, he felt the person who was sent to tell the whole story about the code talkers had arrived. You."

"Me?" I said. "I'm sorry, I'm just a little confused. Are you saying that I should write the code talkers' story? I'm not an author, I have no experience, and if you haven't noticed, I'm not exactly a Navajo."

Carl and Mary were both smiling, then Mary got very serious. "What my husband and about four hundred other Navajos did during the war is probably the best kept secret of World War II. They need someone who has the desire to seek and find the truth about what they did, put it down for the record, and we both believe you are that person."

Write a book. Me? Are they crazy! I wouldn't know where to start, and besides I'm working in the warehouse at Rocky Flats forty hours a week, I'm raising Melinda and … these people have lost their minds! Looking into their faces however, I knew that this was not madness, or a trick. I finally replied, "Okay, how about this, you answer my questions about what they did during the war and I'll consider putting it on paper."

"Well," Mary said, "I think that is fair, but in what form are you going to put their stories?"

"Well," I began, "it might be nice to interview as many code talkers that want their story told, and then print and bind them then give it to them as a record of what they did, so their families will know what they did during the war."

"That sounds like a good place to begin, but it will leave out a lot of background information which will again create more questions than answers. Don't you want to know the whole story?" Mary said.

"Don't the code talkers know it?" I replied.

"No they don't. Carl served in the 2nd Marine Division and how he used the code was different from how code talkers used it in the other divisions. Many articles have been written about the code talkers over the last fifteen years and much of the information is incorrect or incomplete, so telling the story from A to Z is the only way to understand the service they rendered during the war."

This was becoming more complicated by the minute. All I wanted was an answer to my question, and now Mary was talking about me writing the full-fledged story. But, she was right. I did want to know the story from A to Z and nothing less would do. *How the hell did I get myself into this?* I thought about what she said for a few minutes and made my decision, insane as it was.

"First," I said, "are you telling me that no one has ever researched this story from beginning to end?"

Mary replied, "No one has ever taken the time to research this story from beginning to end and it is long overdue. Didn't you say how frustrated you were when you went to the library and looked for the code talkers in all those books and couldn't find any mention of them? Don't you want to know why they were absent?"

"Yes," I said, "it really bothers me that there wasn't anything about them at all, in fact, it made me angry."

"Well," Mary said," there is only one way to remedy that and you are the one to do it."

Crap! Why did she have to be right? How on earth was I going to accomplish this? "Would the code talkers trust me enough to tell me their stories? Where would I find the military proof?" I asked.

Carl finally spoke, "They'll trust you because I do and they are all eager to tell their story. We all need to know the truth."

"The proof," Mary said, "will be harder to find but I'm sure the National Archives will have what you need. I have addresses and phone numbers for about sixty code talkers and I'll give them to you before you leave."

"Who should I start with?" I asked.

"I think Eugene Crawford first, then maybe Wilsie Bitsie." Mary replied.

"Wait a minute! You said you would answer my questions if I agreed to write this story. Are you backing out on me?" I asked.

Mary and Carl both smiled then she said, "No, I'm not going back on my word, but it's getting late and Carl has to teach in the morning. Can you come back tomorrow evening around seven? Feel free to bring your mother and daughter. Carl will be happy to entertain them in his studio." *I want to be entertained by Carl in his studio!*

"I guess that will be okay," I said.

"Well, then we will see you tomorrow night," Mary said.

She walked me to my car, took my hand and said, "This is going to be a great adventure if you are truly brave enough to do it. Carl and I will advise and help you any way we can."

"I appreciate that," I said. "See you tomorrow night." She turned and walked back into the house and I looked at the clock in my car and could barely believe it. It was nearly midnight! Wow, time really does fly when you're having fun. The drive back to Gallup was uneventful but I had a hard time processing what had happened. *Me, write a book?* Well, just because I haven't done it before doesn't mean I can't do it now. Besides, I know that the American public needs to know about the code talkers and I might as well be the one to tell them.

CHAPTER 5

THE FIRST 29

THE NEXT DAY MOM, Melinda, and I decided to go the Hubbell Trading Post located in Ganado. It is one of the oldest trading posts in the entire country and I was curious to see it. I also wanted to have time to process what happened the night before and window-shopping is a perfect venue for idle wanderings.

As we entered Hubbell's, I had the distinct impression that it looked as if it had been part of an old Wild West town. Belts, saddles, and horse blankets were hung from the timbered ceiling. Shelves were lined with canned goods of every variety, beautiful necklaces and rings were displayed on the wall behind the main counter, and jars of candy were stacked in neat rows. Melinda made a beeline for the candy and I allowed her to pick about a dollar's worth. Mom disappeared into the next room and we went after her. *This is paradise!*

The walls were covered with exquisite sandpaintings and hand-woven rugs of all sizes, patterns, and colors. Shelves were lined with intricate pottery, silk-screened t-shirts, and Pendleton blankets. It was almost too much for my eyes to comprehend. It is one of the few times in my life that I wished I had unlimited funds—I wanted one of everything! I settled on a beautiful dark blue t-shirt that had a circular design of Navajo ceremonial dancers. Melinda and Mom chose a similar one and then we headed out to eat lunch. Melinda spotted a sign that advertised "fat sheep" and we had a great laugh about it. We spent the rest of the day wandering around Ganado and Window Rock before heading out for dinner. Since Fort Defiance was fairly close to Ganado, it didn't make sense to drive all the way back to Gallup for supper, then turn around and drive back to the Gormans'.

We arrived at the Gormans' a few minutes before seven and Mom and Melinda were immediately taken to Carl's studio. It was an attached room on the east side of their house and it had a large greenhouse-like ceiling with large windows all around. Several easels held completed or partially completed canvases, the workbench had scattered pieces of pottery, and there was opera music coming from a cassette player. That was not what I was expecting! Carl greeted us and sat Melinda down next to him at his worktable while Mom pulled up an extra chair across from him. Mary led me back toward the living room and closed the studio room door behind her.

Carl Gorman and Melinda McClain, 1994.

"They're in for a really good time," Mary said. "Carl loves to show young children his art and he'll probably let her create something."

"I know she'll appreciate and enjoy that," I said.

We sat at the dining room table and I was anxious to hear the story Mary was about to tell me. I told myself not to interrupt her with questions, as there would be time for that at the conclusion. This time I came prepared with a writing tablet and several good pens. Mary began: "This is what I can reveal to you about 'The First 29'—you might want to take notes. In March of 1942 a Marine Corps recruiter named Frank Shinn came to the reservation and began interviewing Navajos for 'Special Duty' within the Corps. Carl and a number of others wanted to join, partly because jobs were nearly impossible to get, and partly because the Marine Corps was considered an elite organization. Frank did a good job talking up the Corps. Carl was very impressed, not only with Frank, but the uniform he wore. He initially believed that this 'Special Duty' might involve a desk job in Washington, D.C.

"In April, after their interviews, thirty men were chosen and told to report to his office to be transported to Fort Wingate, New Mexico, for lunch and a ceremonial induction into the Marine Corps. From there they would be immediately transported by bus to the Marine Corps Recruit Depot in San Diego, California. On that day only twenty-nine showed up at Frank's office and there are several versions of what happened to the thirtieth man; one was that he got sick, two that he changed his mind, but it was also rumored that whoever this Navajo was he joined later.

"Once this group was taken to the Recruit Depot, they were assigned as the 382nd All American Indian Platoon, the first ever in the Marine Corps." Mary handed me a photograph of the platoon. *This is incredible!* She continued: "They graduated boot camp with some of the highest honors and were immediately transported to Camp Elliott where they were told their 'Special Duty' would begin. They were escorted into a building, down the hall into a classroom with bars on the windows and doors. They were told to relax and that someone would be with them in a moment. Carl remembers it being very quiet and they were all a little nervous.

"A few minutes later an officer entered the room, said he was from the Office of Naval Intelligence, and proceeded to give them a lecture on cryptography, how codes are created and broken, and the military and diplomatic uses of codes. At the conclusion, the officer wrote four rules on a large blackboard:

1. Construct an alphabet.
2. Choose words that are accurate equivalents.
3. Choose short terms for rapid transmission.
4. Memorize all terms.

"He gave them a stern warning not to tell anyone what they were doing unless they wanted to spend the duration of the war in the brig. He told them to try to build a combat dictionary based on their language that could be a weapon the Japanese had no answer for. He left the room and Carl thought the officer was crazy and it was not any version of 'Special Duty' he could have ever imagined. But, they had been trained well as Marines and if this is what they wanted, then they would deliver. They spent the next six weeks developing a combat dictionary based on a modified version of their language and field testing it, and then were divided among the 1st and 2nd Marine Divisions. He was very proud of their accomplishment and believed using the language made him feel protected. He was wounded at Saipan and was stateside when the war ended. He was instructed by his commanding general to not talk about the code until further notice."

There was a long pause and I realized she was finished. I said, "Can I ask a couple of questions?"

"Yes," she replied.

"Where did this idea for using the Navajo language for coded communications come from?"

"Well," she replied, "there are several different versions and I think it's best if you find the true one for yourself."

Crap! I should have seen that one coming! "Okay," I said, "how did Carl use the code during combat?"

"If a request came through for a coded communication then Carl was told to send it in Navajo. It could be reporting an enemy position or calling for artillery fire in a certain place. It depended on how the Commanding Officer wanted it used," she said. *This was fascinating! I wanted to know more ... every detail about the code talkers. I was hooked!*

"So, 'The First 29' created a type of combat dictionary?" I asked.

"Yes," Mary replied. "It was a difficult process because the Navajo language doesn't contain words for things like submarines, grenades, bombs, and the like. Finding an equivalent was hard work, and even though they felt confident about what they created, they had a hard time figuring how exactly it was going to be used."

"Why does Harold doubt 'The First 29'? Is it really a question of jealousy and is he the only one?" I asked.

"I think that because none of the men who followed 'The First 29' were ever told about them, it was easier to not believe, and there are some Navajos who don't think 'The First 29' were smart enough to create it," she replied.

Wow! That surprised me. "So, the success of 'The First 29' made it possible for other Navajos to follow in their footsteps, and as the Marine divisions expanded, they used the code talkers for the duration of the war?" I asked.

"From what I know, the code talkers played a big part during Iwo Jima and Okinawa," Mary continued. "When the war was over, they were all instructed to never talk about the code or what they did with it. The secrecy lasted until 1969 when they were honored at the 4th Marine Division reunion in Chicago. Carl went as the representative for the 2nd Division and others were there representing the remainder of the divisions.

"Philip Johnston was there, and he was telling everyone he was the one who created the code. You can imagine how mad that made Carl! There was an uncomfortable confrontation and it caused some hard feelings. But, that is where the doubt about 'The First 29' began. Philip Johnston was not a part of the code school until after 'The First 29' had been shipped out, so they didn't even know who he was. This is one of the most important things you need to clear up, the code talkers, all of them, need to know exactly how this went down."

I said, "I'd like to know the truth of that myself. I don't like it when people take credit for something they didn't do. There has been far too much of that in our history. To me, Columbus Day is a colossal joke. He didn't know where he was going and didn't know where he was when he arrived and never stepped foot on American soil!" I said.

Mary laughed then said, "Then you know what you have to do. I would suggest you try to speak with Eugene Crawford and Wilsie Bitsie, then go get the military proof. Once they see how serious you are about getting the truth the more cooperation you'll receive."

I thought about what she'd said, and I began getting excited about visiting the National Archives in Washington, D.C. I'd never been back east and thinking about the exciting and revealing documents I might find to help piece the code talker story together was a challenge I couldn't resist.

Mary gave me a copy of the 382nd Platoon photograph, a complete list of the members of 'The First 29,' a copy of the Navajo Tribal Treaty of 1868 and then surprised me by saying, "You have an appointment with Eugene Crawford tomorrow at Nikki's restaurant at noon."

"Where's Nikki's?" I asked. Mary told me it was located on Route 66 close to a McDonald's, not far down the road from my motel. I remembered seeing it on my way into Gallup during my first trip. "Thank you for arranging the meeting. Is there anything specific I should know about Mr. Crawford?" I asked.

"Eugene," Mary replied, "is a very quiet man, but he served with distinction with the Raider Battalions, so you will be safe asking him about that. As to what he will reveal to you is up to him, so let him talk it out before you ask any questions. Wilsie Bitsie might not be so easy to reach. He's turned into somewhat of a recluse, but he is someone you definitely will want to interview. Carl said Wilsie has the best boot camp stories and code school memories, so try to convince him to talk."

"Do you know where he lives?" I asked.

"Red Rock Mobile Home Park just outside of Gallup. I also included the most current addresses for you," Mary replied.

"Thank you for all your help. I really appreciate it. And thank you for welcoming my mom and daughter into your home," I said.

"It was my pleasure," Mary replied.

Melinda burst through the door with a huge smile on her face, telling me that Carl liked what she drew. She put a drawing of a horse in front of me and it was really quite charming. "Good job, this is really nice. Did you have fun with Carl?" I asked. "Yeah, his horses look better than mine but he let me color a mug he is making," she replied. Carl and my mom walked through the door, and I could tell by the expression on Carl's face that he was very pleased with the company he'd had for the last two hours.

"Melinda should continue her art; she has talent," Carl said. *Wow! That is high praise coming from him!*

"She has always been good at coloring, so I will encourage her to continue it," I replied, "Before we go I'm curious about something. Can you explain to me how a full-blooded Navajo ended up with an Irish last name?"

Carl and Mary looked at each other, smiling and laughing, and I knew we were in for a very interesting narrative.

"Well, that's an interesting question and the answer is simple," Carl began. "After the people signed the Treaty of 1868 they were told they had to send their children to school. The army would round them up and escort them to the nearest town where a school had been built. Because none of the children spoke English and none of the soldiers or teachers spoke Navajo, this was a problem. Navajo names are not easy to pronounce and the Anglos didn't seem inclined to learn them.

"The solution was that the soldiers gave each child an Anglo first name, like Tom or Nancy and then gave them their last names. My father was given the name Nelson Gorman and then I was named Carl Nelson Gorman. Of course in many ways that was okay because we like to keep our Navajo names protected from the outside world."

"Then how did Navajo last names like Etsictty, Begay, Yazzie, and Nez come to be?" I asked.

"Well, probably down the generations, they started to keep them, changing only the first name to an Anglo," Mary replied. "Want to know something funny?"

"Absolutely," I replied.

"Every year Carl receives an invitation to attend the Irish Gorman family reunion in Chicago," she stated.

We all looked at each other for a moment then burst out laughing. My wicked sense of humor came pouring out when I said, "Oh Carl, you should go. Dress up in your finest traditional Navajo clothes, put on all your beautiful turquoise jewelry, and walk in there and say, 'Yah-at-tay Gormans, I'm your cousin Carl.'"

We looked at each other for a few seconds, imaging that scene, and it sent us into another laughing fit. We laughed so hard that tears were trickling down our faces. Melinda didn't understand what was so funny, and I told her I would try to explain it later. Mary and Carl hugged all of us, and Mom and Melinda thanked Carl for sharing his art with them.

It was nearly 10:30 p.m. and time to make our way back to Gallup. Mary walked us out to the car and wished me good luck with Eugene and Wilsie. Melinda chatted happily about her time with Carl and I half listened. I was so excited about the interview the next day it was hard to concentrate on what she was saying. I told Mom about the lunch appointment and asked if she wanted to drop me off and go do some more sightseeing with Melinda. Mom said that was fine and they would pick me up around three. My dreams that night were filled with questions I would ask Mr. Crawford and the wonderful answers I would receive. Tomorrow couldn't come fast enough.

EUGENE CRAWFORD

I arrived at Nikki's Restaurant at about five minutes to noon and asked the Navajo hostess if she had seen Mr. Crawford. She smiled and walked me to a booth where he was waiting. I sat down, extended my hand and introduced myself. He was probably in his late seventies to early eighties, wearing a long-sleeved white cotton shirt and jeans, and had a kind, gentle-looking face. "You spoke with Carl?" I asked.

"Yes, he told me to tell you what I remember about the code and the war," he replied. "What do you want to know?"

"Well, if you would, you can start by telling me about boot camp and anything else you feel comfortable telling me," I said. "But first, let's order lunch. Feel free to order anything you want, my treat." He smiled, looked at the menu and then kept adjusting the sleeves of his shirt, and I wondered if he was nervous. He caught me watching him and cleared his throat and said, "Jungle rot."

What? I didn't know how to reply to that statement, so I remained silent. "Got it on Guadalcanal. Got malaria there too," he said. He pulled back the cuff of his shirt and I could see black, scale-like, peeling patches on his wrist and guessed it went all the way up his arms.

"That's a nasty souvenir of the war." I said.

"Yeah, never goes away. Because of the malaria, I can never donate blood. The doc says once you get the parasite, it never leaves. Even Navajo medicine can't cure it," he stated.

I had no idea that malaria had such a long-term effect and it made his sacrifice even greater than I had imagined. Desperate to change the subject, I asked him about boot camp. He smiled and said, "Boot camp was a real interesting experience. The DIs [drill instructors] were tough as nails and reminded me of my grandmother. Your grandmother tells you to do something, you don't argue, you don't ask why, and you better do it before she gets mad."

I laughed and said, "Sounds like Navajo grandmothers are pretty tough."

"Yeah," he continued, "But it helped me through boot camp. You learn discipline at an early age and it never leaves you. Made the DIs crazy that they couldn't rattle us or find hard enough duty to break us. But, I was really good on the firing range. I ended up Expert and most of the platoon did real well."

I was impressed with his matter-of-fact tone and felt we were on common ground, so I ventured to ask him about the code. "Making that code was the hardest thing I ever did. Trying to find terms for all that military equipment made my head ache. We got stuck about two weeks in and John Benally went to ask for help," he stated.

"What kind of help did you need?" I asked.

"Well," he continued, "there were words we didn't know what they were. We all might have graduated from the boarding schools, but I don't think they made us very smart. We needed someone with a better education who might understand some of the terms we struggled with, so Benally talked with the Navy officer in charge and got us some more Navajos. A couple of days later, Ross Haskie, Wilson Price, and Felix Yazzie showed up and we were able to build the rest of the code."

Wait a minute! Three extra Navajos! That means the term "The First 29" really only applies to the boot camp platoon and they really should be known as "The First 32"! I wonder if this kind of truth is what Mary referred to.

"So," I asked, "thirty-two Navajos built the code, not just the original twenty-nine, and the three extra men were already in the Marine Corps?"

"Yeah," he continued, "Ross, Felix, and Wilson had been through boot camp before we got there. I don't know how they found them, but it's a good thing they did. We didn't want to fail the Corps. Wilson had a college education and Ross

Eugene Roanhorse Crawford, Gallup, New Mexico, 1989.

and Felix had a couple of years so they were a lot smarter than the rest of us."

"When you were creating the words did you have any idea how they would be used?" I asked.

"No, not at first. Once a signal officer gave us some sample messages, we started to see how we could put the terms together to make sense. When we got to test them on the field radios, the officers got real confused because they couldn't figure out how we sent the message in Navajo and got it in English at the other end," he replied.

I was totally amazed. He went on to explain, "The Navajo language doesn't have words for things like submarine, hand grenade, tank, battleship, or bazooka. It doesn't change to suit the outside world, so if a word doesn't serve a purpose in their everyday or spiritual life, they don't invent one. Finding a Navajo word that would fit the unfamiliar word was hard but when we did, it made sense."

"Can you give me an example?" I asked.

"Well, like submarine, we just called it an iron fish. Tank looked like a turtle and a grenade looked like a potato so we used the Navajo words for them. It was easy to memorize and everyone knew that if a message included a 'turtle' it meant they were calling for tank support," he stated.

I listened with rapt attention, not wanting to miss a single word. "Carl said you served with a Raider Battalion, which one?" I asked.

"I served with Carlson's and it was pretty good duty," he replied. "All of the men respected what we did and we never felt different from any other Raider. The additional training was hard. I earned my Para Marine wings."

"Para Marine, what's that?" I asked.

"Well, you had to do six jumps out of a plane to qualify. It scared me to death, but I did it anyway. When the brass found out, they put a stop to it right away. Guess they didn't want code talkers jumping out of planes with a chance of getting smashed up on the landing," he said.

"My dad served in the Navy and one of the things I remember him saying was 'You don't ever jump out of a perfectly good airplane unless it's on fire and going down.'"

Eugene smiled and said, "Well, he was probably right, but falling out of the sky, then gently going down after the chute opens is the closest to flying like a bird I'll ever get. Mother Earth looks a lot different from above." We finished our lunch in relative silence and I was formulating what questions to ask next. Suddenly he looked at me and said in a flat voice, "War is a strange thing. The elders would tell us stories about fighting with the Spanish and other tribes, but they never told you how ugly it really is. And dirty. It was dirty everywhere. You could never quite get the dirt and sweat off of you. I don't remember seeing a single green thing the whole time I was in the Pacific. Once you were in combat, you had to learn how to forage for extra food. Supply lines were not real good and sometimes we had to make do with what we could find. Carlson was real strict about keeping our feet dry, said we couldn't do our good job with bad feet. Problem was the air was so wet, it was hard to dry any of our clothing, but my feet are fine to this day because of his rules."

"How did you feel about using the code?" I asked.

He smiled and said, "It was great. It always made me feel protected when I sent a message in Navajo. Japs didn't like it, always tried to confuse us by screaming and yelling in our ears, but we were confident in our code and disciplined enough to get the message through."

"How did they get access to your radio lines?" I asked.

"We heard they crawled through our lines at night and put tracer wires on our lines so they could listen in. They were smart. They were tough and they fought like demons. Nothing they taught us in boot camp prepared us for that," he said.

"Was it strange to be so far from home?" I asked. He looked out of the window for a few minutes before replying.

"Yeah, that part of Mother Earth is so different from here. I'd never seen the ocean until boot camp and then getting on one of those big ships was a little scary. Using my language made me feel better about being so far away from home, and the people I met on leave made it easier.

"After Guadalcanal, we got ten days leave on New Zealand and when we got there, the people cheered and a band played. They made us feel real important. Then an older man approached me and asked me what tribe I belonged to. I was real surprised, but I told him I was Navajo and he insisted that I go home with him. He was with about ten other people. I didn't want to be rude, so I went with him. We drove about twenty miles out to the country, he didn't say anything along the way and I was real curious where he was taking me.

"We arrived at his place, it looked like a little village and a lot of people came up to the car. I got out and they started talking, real excited. The older man told me this was a village of Maori, native people of New Zealand. He took me inside his house and gave me the best bed and asked if I was hungry. This was a real strange experience, when the people were talking I could understand some of what they were saying. Later I attended one of their ceremonies and they were a lot like the ones we had. Here I was, so far away from home and there were people that had ceremonies I could recognize … it was the strangest thing that ever happened to me during the war. I heard later that a couple more code talkers stayed with the Maori and they said the same thing. Makes you wonder how that happened to be."

I was surprised, to say the least. To think that almost half a world away, two very different native peoples had the ability to understand each other.

Lunch was over, and I saw Mom pull into the parking lot, so I asked him if there was anything else he wanted to tell me. "No, but are you going to talk to Wilsie?" he asked.

"I'm going to try. Why?" I said.

He smiled and said, "Wilsie knows more about the code than almost anyone and he has some great boot camp stories. He was a Raider too and served in a lot more battles than I did."

"I'll definitely try to interview him. I want to thank you for your service during the war and for taking the time to speak with me. I know it wasn't easy to recall," I said.

He smiled and said, "You're a good listener. Are you going to tell our story?" he asked.

"That's what I plan on doing. If I have more questions, would you be willing to meet with me again?" I asked.

"Yeah, I can do that," he replied. We got up and left the restaurant and I got in the car and asked Mom and Melinda how their day went. The conversation back to the motel was a blur. I was still trying to digest all that Eugene had told me. I couldn't wait to call Mary and tell her about my conversation with Eugene.

Mom and Melinda decided to lie down for a nap and I called Mary. She seemed very pleased about my meeting with Eugene and glad that he was so cooperative. She suggested I call her daughter Zonnie and share the information I had gathered. Zonnie was in the process of filming a documentary about "The First 29" and we could help each other out. She also thought it might be a good idea for the both of us to go to Washington, D.C. and visit the National Archives together. "That sounds like a wonderful idea. I would be happy to share the information with her. Where does she live?" I asked.

"She's in school in Phoenix. I'll give you her phone number and you can call her when you get home," Mary said.

Mary gave me Zonnie's phone number and I ended the call. Tomorrow I was going to go to the mobile home park and try to see Wilsie Bitsie. Hopefully he would be as cooperative as Carl and Eugene had been.

The next day, I dropped Mom and Melinda off in Gallup and we arranged to meet back up in about two hours. I got directions to the mobile home park at a gas station and drove out there. Mary had provided me with his address, and his trailer wasn't hard to find. It was a well-kept house with a large porch, and American and Marine Corps flags were hanging from a pole in the front yard. There weren't any vehicles in sight but I decided to knock on the door and take my chances. I knocked several times and waited for about five minutes with no response. I was disappointed, but I would just have to try later. I knew that I would be making many more trips back here and hopefully we could connect with each other.

It was time to go home. This trip had been eye-opening, fascinating, puzzling, and intriguing. Mary was right. I opened a door that created more questions than I currently had answers for. But, I was excited to be on this journey and anxious to connect with Zonnie.

It was good to be home! A couple of days later, I read the Treaty of 1868 and was saddened that much of what our government promised the Navajos, they have never honored. For example, one teacher for every twenty-five students, hell…they don't even come close to that. When I got to the last page, I saw a number of signatures and Mary had attached a Post-it note that said "Count the names." So I started counting.

Wow! A tsunami of goose bumps enveloped my entire body. *Twenty-nine … twenty-nine Navajo elders signed the treaty that allowed the Navajo people to return to their ancestral land. This was no coincidence!* I started to laugh … *these* Navajos were the original "First 29!" I immediately called Mary and found myself still laughing. When I repeated my observation she began laughing too. "How many more goose-bump-giving moments am I in for?" I asked.

"Who knows," she replied. She asked me if I had spoken to Zonnie yet, and I said I was going to call her in a couple of days. We said good night and I went to bed still seeing the twenty-nine Navajo names on the treaty in my mind.

I called Zonnie about four days after we returned and we began a friendship that exists to this day. She is articulate, intelligent, and just as invested in learning the truth about the code talkers as I was. I told her about my conversations with Eugene Crawford, Dean Wilson, Bill Toledo, Tom Begay, and John Kinsel. She laughed when I related how Dean scolded me about not writing down what they were saying. She definitely thought a trip to D.C. would be great, and said she would keep in touch and let me know how we could arrange the logistics. Zonnie, like me, was a single parent, but she had three boys to my one girl. Coordinating this trip would be a little tricky, but I could hardly wait.

During our conversations over the next few months, we exchanged information about our childhoods, parenting issues, and things we had learned about the code talkers. I asked her if she knew how many Navajos signed the Treaty of 1868.

"No, why?" she said.

"There were twenty-nine," I replied. There was such a long pause, I thought she hung up on me. "Zonnie? Are you there?"

"I'm here. Are you sure about that?" she asked.

"Well, I have a copy in front of me and there are definitely twenty-nine names on the treaty," I said.

"That is so … so … weird!" she stated.

"Yeah, gave me a huge wave of goose bumps," I said. "Me too," she replied.

She then went on to graciously share with me her interview with Frank Shinn. He was the Marine Corps recruiter responsible for compiling the members of "The First 29" and the second all-Navajo platoon in 1943. He greatly admired the Navajo people and even though he never knew at the time the men he recruited and helped induct became the famous code talkers, he was nonetheless proud to have been a part of the "Pilot Project." We were both anxious to get to D.C. and find documentation of the code talkers for our projects.

To pass the time, I decided to go back to the library and research more about the South Pacific conflict. Only this time, it would be to learn the reasons behind Japan's actions and perhaps learn why the Marines needed code talkers. I needed to understand what the code talkers lived through in order to know why they were necessary. Besides, I didn't know as much about the South Pacific campaigns as I did about the European and it was time I did.

What I learned over the next four months was fascinating, disturbing, puzzling, and hard to swallow. The Japanese sought to control all of Asia in the same manner that Hitler sought to control all of Europe. It was scary to see how closely aligned their ideologies were, how both leaders thought they were superior to all other races of people and that it was perfectly acceptable to conquer, subjugate, slaughter, and rule the "unworthy masses." America was eventually forced to fight on two very different fronts. It gave me a greater understanding of what our armed forces faced, and I was humbled by the manner in which they conducted themselves. The Americans who faced the Japanese were forced to fight an enemy who did not value life on either side, an idea I have never understood. I hadn't realized what fanaticism looked like, and it certainly was anything but appealing.

How did such insanity ever come to fruition? I realized I might never find an adequate answer on that count, so I stayed focused and absorbed as much information as I could.

But now, it was time to start planning a trip to Washington, D.C. with Zonnie, and I was really looking forward to this next leg of the code talker journey.

CHAPTER 6

THE ARCHIVES

THROUGH MANY PHONE CALLS OVER THE NEXT SIX MONTHS, Zonnie and I decided to travel to Washington, D.C., during the second week in March 1990. Mary arranged for us to stay with family friends, Susan and Jerry Bernstein, and we coordinated our flights so we could connect with each other in Denver before going on to D.C. I made arrangements for Melinda to stay with my mom and sister Dona and promised to bring her back some great souvenirs. I realized I would be there for my fortieth birthday and couldn't imagine a better present than finding great piles of documents relating to the code talkers.

Driving through Washington, D.C. is the most frustrating experience I have ever had. After the British burned the place to the ground in 1812, the founding fathers redesigned it so you could not take a straight path to either the White House or the Capitol. Trying to figure out the streets to take to our destination was an exercise in extreme patience! Streets had roundabouts, and you had to stay in the correct lane in order not to be forced to turn down a one-way street and end up hopelessly lost. As confusing as it was, I noticed there was a very different feel to this place. I told Zonnie that the energy felt old, ancient … almost heavy. She said she felt that way too, but after all, this was one of the oldest cities in the country so it should feel this way.

"There are places on the rez that feel this way," she stated. "Really, where?" I asked.

"Canyon de Chelly, Navajo Mountain, Crystal Mountain, and especially Kaibeto. We need to visit the Marine Corps Memorial, and I'd like to visit Ira Hayes's grave in Arlington Cemetery," she replied.

Zonnie Gorman, Washington, D.C., 1990.

Ira Hayes ... he helped raise the replacement flag on Iwo, but was he a Navajo? "Was Ira a Navajo?" I asked.

"No, he was Pima, but most of the code talkers either attended school with him or knew him in the Corps. My Dad said to come and pay my respects, so that's what I need to do," she replied.

"When an elder asks, you comply," I stated.

"Yep," she said. "I went through a special cleansing and protection ceremony, so I won't bring back any traces from the cemetery. I really dislike it because it means I can't bathe for another three days," she said.

Wow! I still had a lot to learn about Navajo culture. We finally arrived at the Bernsteins' home and settled in for the night. I wanted to get to the archives first thing in the morning. We only had three working days to find some documentation and I didn't want to waste a minute. The next morning we got up, had coffee and a bagel, and set out for the archives before the rest of the household was awake. The two-hour time difference, three for Zonnie, was a little rough at first, but my desire to get my hands on military documentation overrode the jet lag. I found a free parking place a block from the archives and we walked the distance in silence. The clouds in the sky were a beautiful shade of pink and squirrels were running everywhere.

There are a number of things that make me truly proud to be an American, but at the top of that list is our National Archives. Entering that building and searching the card catalogs left me with such a sense of awe. It should be mandatory for every citizen to visit the archives once in their lifetime, pick a subject at random, and see what a vast store of knowledge this country has generated. It was truly breathtaking. It was also a little bit intimidating and overwhelming. We had no idea where to start. So, as usual I went straight to the help desk and asked where to find information about the code talkers. The archivist looked at me like I just stepped off a flying saucer.

This can't be good! If the archivists don't know where to look then how am I ever going to find the documentation? A moment later, she regained her composure and asked where they might have served. I told her they were Marines, communication personnel, and served in the South Pacific. She went to her computer and typed in something, wrote it down, and then handed me the paper with a box number on it. She instructed me where to take it and that once the box was located, I would have access to it in the research room. The wait, she warned me, might be about half an hour long. I thanked her, and Zonnie and I went into the research room to wait for the box. The atmosphere was the same as it is in any library, hushed and sedate, so we talked in low voices, speculating about what we might find.

We had only been waiting about twenty minutes when an attendant walked in and placed a box at the desk where we were sitting. I must have stared at it for what seemed like a very long time before Zonnie nudged me and told me to open it. I took a deep breath, exhaled slowly, and opened it. Inside there were four fat manila file folders and as I opened the first one, I couldn't have been more disappointed!

After reading the entire contents, all the documents inside were all about communication regulations, rules, and reports about Morse code messages.

I gave the file to Zonnie and said, "There isn't anything in here about the code talkers, but maybe we'll get lucky with the next one." The next folder held one very interesting report that had nothing to do with the code talkers, but revealed an episode that occurred during World War I involving Choctaw Indians. The SRH-120 report stated Choctaws used their language to confuse the enemy in order to affect a safe withdrawal of allied troops trapped behind enemy lines in France. I handed it to Zonnie and said, "This is absolutely fascinating. Read it and let me know what you think."

She read the report and said, "This is fascinating, I had no idea something like this happened during World War I. Maybe this is where the Marines got the idea for the code talkers. Is there anything else in there?" I scanned the rest of the documents but found nothing of value. I unfastened the folder, pulled out the report, and took it to the copy machine. I definitely wanted a copy of this and hoped down the line it might be of use. The rest of the material in the box held no useful information, so I took it back to the attendant. I asked if they had enrollment records for the Marine Corps, and she replied that they had muster rolls for all the branches of service and would I like to see them? I asked Zonnie if she thought we should look through them and see if we could find any Navajo names and she agreed it was worth a shot. I requested the Marine Corps muster rolls from January 1940 to 1942 to begin with.

The muster rolls are fascinating records. They list the complete name, rank, and serial number of everyone who enlisted or was drafted into the Marines. As we started down the lists, we got excited every time we recognized a Navajo name. Zonnie had the good sense to bring a list of known code talkers with her and we started writing down service serial numbers after locating their names. I was amazed how many we found in just that one afternoon. Time flew by and we were ready to call it a day.

On the drive back we chatted excitedly about the SRH-120 report and the many names we were able to verify from the muster rolls. It had been a good day. Jerry told some wonderful stories about Carl and Mary, and then showed me some paintings that he'd bought—they were Carl's but they had a different signature. I asked him about it and he said, "There was a period of time when Carl signed some of his work with his Navajo name: Kin-ya-ooney-beyeh, son of Kin-ya-ooney."

"Wow that is fascinating." I replied. We spent the rest of the evening in general chatter, and then called it a night.

The next day Zonnie said she had errands to run, so she dropped me off at the archives and would meet me after lunch. I continued scanning the muster rolls and found really interesting notations about certain types of misconduct and its consequences. But I wanted to find more, so I went up to one of the archivists and asked where I could find more Marine Corps records.

She informed me that the majority of those records were kept at the Suitland Branch in Maryland. She seemed a little put out because the National Archives had a backdated order for the Marine Corps to release them to the Archives and they had still not complied.

I asked where I could find combat photos and she sent me to the fourth floor. I searched the catalogs and found a number of photos to look at. I wrote down my request, waited about a half an hour, donned a pair of white cotton gloves, and viewed them. It was strange, because they all seemed to be posed, instead of action shots, but they were all good, and I was elated when I found one of Carl on Saipan. I also researched Pacific island photos I knew I would need for the book. There were really interesting ones of Bougainville, Guadalcanal, and Iwo Jima. These islands looked so much more sinister in black and white. I wrote down the numbers and how many copies I wanted, and turned in my request along with the payment. I would receive them in about six weeks.

Knowing I would have to go to the Suitland Archives to find what I was looking for, I asked where it was located. I was told it was just across a bridge not far from here. We would be leaving in two days and I made up my mind that another trip back here would be necessary. Today was my birthday and I wanted to celebrate it with a nice dinner. The trip had been very rewarding and more than I expected. We returned to the house, got dressed, and Zonnie and I headed for a little neighborhood Italian restaurant. I had the most delicious lasagna I have ever eaten and a glass of white wine, and the waiters sang "Happy Birthday" to me. All in all, it was one of my better birthdays.

Saturday afternoon was one of those rainy, misty, cool days and we decided it would be the perfect atmosphere to visit Arlington National Cemetery. We checked in at the visitors office and asked for the location of Ira Hayes's grave. After looking at the map and getting ourselves oriented, we started walking in the direction laid out on the map. We didn't talk; Arlington is a place where quiet reverence is an unspoken rule. Winding through the paths and checking the map, we finally located his marker. I knew very little about Ira Hayes, so I stayed on the path while Zonnie walked up to his marker. I closed my eyes and said a silent prayer of thanks for all who gave their lives in defense of our way of life. Arlington can be emotionally overwhelming. Seeing the thousands upon thousands of white markers brings home the fact that war, no matter what the justification, is all around a bad idea. We walked in silence through the cemetery and looked for the Marine Corps Memorial. Checking the map, we discovered it was just outside the cemetery boundary, so we made our way towards it.

Pictures do not do justice to this magnificent work of art. It is awe inspiring in its scope and detail and the bronze figures appeared as if they would finish raising the flag and then step down from the base. I got waves of goose bumps walking around it, seeing the inscriptions of the history of the Corps going all the way back to the Revolutionary War. Like the Archives, this memorial should be viewed in person to receive its full effect. I took a few pictures and we made our way back to the car. Words were unnecessary, as we were both filled with all kinds of emotions and probably couldn't have expressed them if we tried.

The Bernsteins were having a small dinner party and it was great to socialize with people who knew Carl and Mary from a different time and shared those memories. Carl, it turns out, is quite the prankster and he enjoyed teasing people to see how "tolerant" they really were. It was great fun and I really enjoyed their hospitality. Staying in motels can be lonely and solitary, so staying in the Bernsteins' home was a real treat.

The trip back home was uneventful, and Zonnie and I had plenty of time to recount what we'd discovered. She changed planes in Denver and we hugged and said we would keep in touch. I was anxious to get home and tell my family what I'd discovered. Besides, I knew I had more birthday presents waiting for me.

Over the next couple of months, I began putting the background information on Japan and the island battles on paper. It meant many more trips back to the library to outline those events, but I was learning so much that it was worth the effort. I also decided that another trip to the D.C. area was an absolute necessity. I planned to go the second week in July and spend an entire week researching and I wasn't coming home empty-handed. I went back and looked at the three documents the Historical Center sent me and noticed that there were a series of numbers on them. Maybe they would mean something to the archivists. I could only hope they would lead me to what I needed to find.

The next few months flew by. I was in constant phone contact with Mary and Zonnie and we went over the SRH-120 report with a fine-tooth comb. We speculated on what it meant and perhaps what its usefulness was to the Marines during their search for a code the Japanese couldn't break. I was so mentally stimulated by these two intelligent women and really eager to find documentation and then get back to the rez to interview more code talkers.

SUITLAND ARCHIVES, DAY 1

I arrived in the Washington, D.C. area the second week in July and looked forward to diving into the Marine Corps records. However, the summer weather in D.C. was a real shock. The high humidity almost suffocated me—the air was so wet you could drink it with a straw. Driving to Suitland, Maryland, was another road adventure as the streets were marked incorrectly and I got lost twice. After finally managing to find the right street, it turned out to be a straight shot to the location. I have always had a great sense of direction. Rarely do I ever get lost or turned around, but the streets of D.C. and Suitland were trying my patience!

I checked in at the reception desk and asked to speak with an archivist. A young woman came out and after introductions, I asked her where would be a good place to start to find documents about the code talkers. She gave me the same blank expression I experienced from the archivist at the National Archives: deer in the headlights. I pulled out one of the documents I brought with me and asked if the numbers made any sense to her. After she looked at it she said, "This record group is one that belongs with commandant of the Marine Corps records and if I'm not mistaken the sub number is one that belongs to the communication records." Music to my ears!

"Can I begin a search with the communication records starting in 1940?" I asked.

"I'll get a list of those and you can start pulling them but you can only have five boxes at a time," she replied.

"That will be a great start. Thanks for all your help."

She showed me how to request the record group, told where the research room was located, and instructed me that I could not bring anything into the room except blank paper, pencils, and a debit card for the copy machine. There were lockers with keys lining the hallway where I could store my purse. It cost a quarter to open the locker but it would be refunded when I was ready to leave.

I found an empty locker and stowed my purse and the documents I brought with me, but kept out the legal tablet, pencils, and the debit card, then walked into the room. I handed my request to the desk attendant, found a seat at an empty table, and waited for my first delivery. My stomach was wriggling in anticipation of what I was about to discover, so I looked around the room to distract myself. There were shelves along one of the walls that held some very interesting books so I browsed until I heard the sound of a cart entering the room. The attendant waved to me, I signed for the five boxes, and then took the cart back to my seat.

I sat down, took a couple of deep breaths to calm myself, and opened the first box. It contained five rather fat manila folders and my hands shook a little as I pulled out the first one. At the top of my tablet, I wrote down the access and file folder numbers in case I found something I needed to copy. I also remembered I would need to correctly footnote any documents I ended up using for the book. The third document down was the same one the Historical Center sent me, so I knew I was on the right trail. Then I found four more with references to the code talkers and noticed they had other numbers listed at the top. I reasoned that these were some type of cross-reference to other record groups so I wrote them all down for further inspection. I began pulling them out and copying them, careful to make sure they were put back in their proper order and continued until I finished the first folder. I set the copies aside and dove into the next folder.

To my dismay, the rest of the folders and all five boxes held nothing, so I submitted another request for the next series of boxes within that record group and then another series. *Crap! Crap! Crap!* By the end of that day I had found nothing! I was getting discouraged, so I went to a different record group and again found nothing in the first three boxes. The day was drawing to a close, and I decided to pack it in and start fresh tomorrow.

This was not a good feeling. What if I didn't find what I needed? Where else could I possibly look? I normally don't get frustrated, but not finding anything on the code talkers was really starting to bother me. I could only hope that tomorrow would deliver something … anything on them.

Returning to Suitland the next day, the heat and humidity seemed to be lower, and I was cautiously optimistic about the day's search. I decided to investigate a new record group with the hope it would put me on a more rewarding trail.

The boxes arrived and I opened the first one. As I pulled out the first fat folder, I held my breath. *Crap! Nothing!* Everything in those five boxes was a dud. I requested the next series of boxes and continued my search. *Nothing!* I decided to take a long lunch and left the archives with a disappointed heart. When I returned, an archivist stopped me and asked how my search was going. "Not very well, at the moment," I replied.

"I think you need to check out this record group and start with January 1942. You might just find what you're looking for," she replied.

She handed me a record group number I was not familiar with. "Thanks for your help. I'll have it pulled now."

"Good luck," she said.

As I was to discover, this record group was also directly related to the commandant of the Marine Corps. The very first document held a list of Navajo recruits with names, ranks, and serial numbers. *JACKPOT!* Forgetting where I was, and not realizing I was speaking out loud, I let out a hard, hushed, "Yes!" I immediately clapped my hand over my mouth and looked around the room. Several people were giving me dirty looks and the attendant motioned me to come to her desk. Like a child who had been caught speaking out of turn in class, I sheepishly walked up to her. In a whisper I said, "I'm sorry for that outburst. I didn't realize I said that out loud."

"Well," said the attendant, "you need to be more aware. I think you need to step outside and compose yourself."

"Uh … okay," I replied.

I walked really fast down the hallway and burst outside, all the while trying to contain my sense of elation, but it was useless. I started dancing around with gleeful abandon at what I had found. Then I saw several people looking out the windows of the research room, shaking their heads at my unbridled dance of what I'm sure they considered total lunacy. I couldn't have cared less what they thought. They didn't know me or my frustration from the day before, so I just smiled and waved.

After a few more minutes I was able to contain myself and went back into the building. I stopped at the desk and apologized again for my outburst. As I walked back to the table, I took a deep breath and began reading the document. Page after page contained at least ten Navajo recruits and one document had five of them coming out of Texas. The letter stated that the Army had signed up the Navajos and the Marine Corps recruiter was furious. He made it sound like the Army was poaching and was not pleased about it. He was requesting the commandant to intercede and make the Army release the Navajos into his custody. The next document contained the commandant's reply that resulted in the Corps being allowed to secure the Navajos the Army had recruited.

As I went through the rest of the documents, it appeared that every Navajo recruit reported directly to the commandant, but why? At that moment the *why* didn't matter. I was sure I would learn the answer to that question later, but I was so thrilled at this discovery that I just copied what I needed and kept on going.

Another folder revealed the demonstration transcript Philip Johnston arranged, his recruitment proposal, and letters from Major General Clayton B.

Vogel. By the looks of it, Vogel was the one that created the idea of the Pilot Project, a transcript of a meeting with Marine Corps brass and the BIA (Bureau of Indian Affairs). That one really threw me for a loop. Why would the Marine Corps have to conduct a meeting with the BIA? I couldn't think about that at the moment. The day was running out and I had to get as much material copied as possible. A bell sounded and an announcer stated that the archives were closing. I closed up the folder and put it back in the box. I asked the attendant how to recall the material. She told me to put my name on a blank piece of paper on top of the boxes and put the cart along the wall, and I could retrieve it tomorrow.

The drive back to my motel was a blur. I had so many questions swirling through my head that I thought it would burst. I couldn't wait to call Mary and tell her what I'd found. I ate supper at a little diner that featured barbeque and honestly, it was the best I had ever tasted. Back in the room, I began sorting by date the documents I'd copied. I sat down and started reading a few of them, making a list of questions that arose and stopped only when I needed a bathroom break. I only got part of the way through the fifty I had copied, so I decided to wait until tomorrow to call Mary. There was so much I just wanted to read and I was tired when my head hit the pillow.

SUITLAND ARCHIVES, DAY 2

I opened the folder I had viewed the day before, relating to the documents on Philip Johnston's demonstration. As I went into the last box, dated January 1943–1945, I came across letters that startled me.

It appeared that someone had leaked information about the code talkers to the *San Diego Union* newspaper. There was an investigation, and the code school instructors, along with Johnston, were given a warning that this project was "Secret" and no information was to be given any member of the press. Then I found a letter regarding another article that had been printed in the *Arizona Highways* magazine. This entire article outlined the code talker program. I was stunned! This was a serious breach of security. The letter informed the instructors and Johnston that an investigation would commence and the guilty parties would be punished.

Philip Johnston explained that the editor of the magazine was a friend of his and what he told him was "off the record." The Navajo instructors stated they never spoke with the editor and had no idea who might have leaked information about their program. I would have to try to find further information from someone about Philip Johnston.

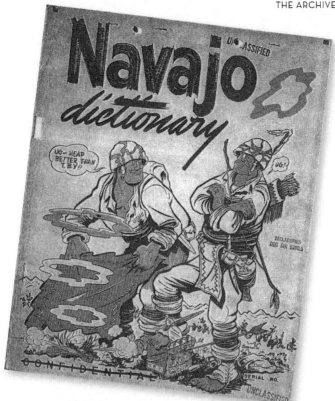

Cover of the Navajo Dictionary, Suitland Archives.

After finishing the first five boxes, I then requested the next five from the list the archivist provided. These were a little disappointing. They didn't contain as much information as I would have liked, but they did give me three other record groups to search. I requested the next one and found more information about the type of communications the Navajos were requested to send. I also found letters of praise from field commanders, class schedules, and then the big one … a copy of the Navajo Dictionary!

I held it in my hand for a long time before I opened it. The cover was so offensive to me that I had a hard time getting past it. Judge for yourself and see if you find it as objectionable as I do. I opened it and began reading. I would definitely have to have Wilsie explain how this came about. I copied it and continued on with the search. I found many more letters of commendation regarding the code talkers and copied all of them. At this point, I was going to copy anything and everything that had to do with them.

By the end of my trip, I'd managed to amass about one hundred and fifty documents. If I had been able to find even this much, why hadn't the Historical Center? I couldn't wait to get home and call Mary and Zonnie and share what I had discovered. This had been an excellent adventure, but I knew that I would need to try to find some regular Marines that served with the code talkers to fill in some of the blanks. But, that could wait until I got home. I spent the last day shopping for souvenirs and visiting the Smithsonian Museum and Mount Vernon. I wanted to absorb as much of this country's oldest historical places as possible, and besides, they were absolutely fascinating.

During the plane ride, I started reading through some of the documents and the one about the meeting with the BIA really set my teeth on edge. The condescending tone of their comments gave the impression that they viewed the Navajos in a very unflattering light, as if they were witless children that had to be tended to in all matters. But their conclusions about using the Navajo language for coded communications was applauded and approved, so I guessed this must have been one of the reasons the Marine Corps wanted to use it.

There were a thousand questions running through my mind and the only way they would be answered was by the code talkers themselves. I knew I would have to make another trip to the rez, and soon. I would also have to find a way to contact Marines who served with them.

Wait a minute! Idiot! My brother David was a Marine, so he might be able to help me. I put the documents back in my briefcase and took a quick nap. There would be time enough to sort and read through them once I got home.

CHAPTER 7

QUESTIONS AND ANSWERS

I PUT ALL THE DOCUMENTS IN CHRONOLOGICAL ORDER and read them thoroughly; putting Post-it notes with questions on the ones I had to figure out. I called Mary the second day after I returned and related some of the information. She suggested that I send her and Zonnie copies of everything, so that they would have them on hand when I called. I agreed, and told her I would call her in about a week, so she would have time to digest the information.

I started planning another trip that would coincide with the Gallup Inter-Tribal Indian Ceremonial taking place August 12th through the 15th. I also had a great conversation with my brother David and he said that during his boot camp training, the code talkers had been briefly mentioned. That surprised me. Then he suggested I put a request for Marines who might have served with code talkers in *Leatherneck* magazine, the "bible" for past and present members of the Corps. So, I formulated a request for any Marine who had knowledge of or had served with the code talkers to please contact me and sent it off. I didn't know if I would get any responses but I hoped I would at least get a few. It turned out that the few that did respond divulged stories that became a great transition for the code talker story.

HENRY AND ALICE HISEY

A couple of weeks after I placed my request in *Leatherneck*, I received a wonderful letter from Henry Hisey. He told me he served with code talkers Teddy Draper and James Cohoe in the 5th Marine Division and he would be happy to share those experiences with me. He and Teddy had remained close friends over the years, visiting each other's hometowns and sharing camping trips on the

Henry and Alice Hisey, Washington, D.C., 1995.

reservation. I wanted to interview him for the book and asked him if that would be possible. They lived in Virginia, so I offered to come and visit them the next time I traveled to Suitland. He and his wife Alice said it would be acceptable and looked forward to meeting me in person.

In the meantime, we carried on weekly conversations about Henry's experiences during the war. He was open, funny, and had a great perspective about the war. These people became two of my new best friends and I enjoyed our conversations. Henry's recollections would be a valuable addition to the code talker story. I looked forward to meeting Henry and Alice in person and hoped his further recollections would be of value to the story. Either way, it was wonderful to be able to meet with a Marine who served on Iwo Jima.

RICHARD BONHAM

Among the other responses was one from Richard Bonham, who stated that he was a foxhole buddy with Bill Toledo. They were assigned to the Headquarters and Service Company, 27th Regiment, 3rd Marine Division. They served together on Bougainville, Guam, and Iwo Jima. He offered to give me a more detailed record of his recollections and asked if a tape would suffice. He lived in California, so a trip there to interview him in person was not feasible. I was thrilled with his offer and sent him a letter thanking him for his help, and saying that I would greatly appreciate anything he wanted to reveal about his time with Bill Toledo. This was a major coup!

He called me a couple of days later to say the tape was in the mail, and if I had any questions, I could call him. He then related that in 1981, he attended a special presentation involving the code talkers at Camp Pendleton and approached a couple of female Navajos.

"I asked them if they knew Bill Toledo and they said they did, but they heard he passed away. My heart dropped. We had been so close during the war and I felt so terrible that we had lost touch with each other after the war. As I walked around the bus they'd arrived in, I ran smack into him! I couldn't speak for a moment. We looked at each other and immediately hugged. Tears were in both our eyes as we stood there. It was wonderful!

"After that we kept in touch and attended annual reunions with the surviving members of the 27th Regiment. We all had a close connection and having Bill be a part of our reunions made them that much more special."

I thanked him for his time and looked forward to hearing what he'd recorded. Listening to his tape, he said something that absolutely floored me. He said that Bill had been separated from the unit and was marched, at gunpoint, by a nervous Marine who believed him to be a Japanese infiltrator to their commanding officer's location. The commanding officer then assigned the protection of Bill to Richard, his "unofficial bodyguard." This unsettled me, so I called Richard for clarification.

"Good afternoon Richard, I have just a couple of questions and it would be terrific if you can take the time to answer them for me," I said.

"No problem, Sally. How can I help you," he replied.

"On your tape you stated that your commanding officer assigned you to be a bodyguard for Bill. I find that extraordinary and puzzling. Can you enlighten me?" I asked.

There was a short pause before he answered. "Well, I guess some Marines didn't know what a Navajo looked like, and thought Bill was Japanese. The Japs had a habit of sneaking into food lines dressed in uniforms they'd taken from dead Marines, so it was a bit of a problem. You must understand, the enemy was very recognizable; they had dark hair, dark eyes, and skin that wasn't white, and unfortunately Bill fit that description. Because his code became so valuable as the battle raged on, the entire unit vowed to make sure nothing happened to Bill. Of course, he never knew anything about being guarded."

"That's amazing," I replied. "Is that why you reacted in such a gruff manner when Bill got away from your protection on Guam?"

He laughed. "Yes, that was a very sticky situation. Bill was given an order, which he obeyed without question. We laugh about it now, but it was very serious at the time. If anything had happened to him, it would have carried serious consequences for me."

"I wonder how many other code talkers had bodyguards?" I said.

"I'm guessing that many did, especially the ones near the front lines. However, it was probably an individual command decision. I never heard any scuttlebutt, but they were secret, so I'm only venturing a guess here," he replied.

"Well, thank you for clearing that up, you've been very kind and helpful. Take care." I said.

"Call me if you need anything else," he said.

Richard Bonham was that first to confirm to me that many of the code talkers had bodyguards and explain the reasons why they were necessary.

LOREN MYRING

Loren Myring's response stated that he served with a code talker named Willie Notah and they were great buddies. He said that Willie was a quiet but efficient Marine and the messages he sent on Iwo saved a lot of lives. He didn't go into much more detail about Willie's code-talking duties. His letter ended with the event that took Willie's life on Iwo Jima.

"We were stationed at the base of Hill 382 when a mortar attack began. We scrambled for cover, but Willie was in the middle of sending a message for support when a round hit just in front of him. His body flew up in the air, his left leg was blown away, and he died instantly. The real heroes of any war are always the ones who never make it home."

Tears slid down my face at his recollection. Here was the first eyewitness account of a code talker who died in combat performing his duty to the last minute of his life. Loren and I kept in touch and I made sure he received a copy of the book.

J. P. BERKELEY

J. P. Berkeley was the first and only high-ranking Marine Corps officer who replied to my request. His information tied together the beginnings of the Pilot Project and the meeting with the BIA, and gave credit for it to the right person: Major General Clayton B. Vogel. His recollections were just about what I expected from a former officer—formal and to the point. He was assigned to the communications division, so his information was crucial and I was able to match it with the documents I'd found. We corresponded with each other a few more times when I had questions about the documents and he was always gracious and helpful. He was delighted and thrilled after he read the book. He felt the story was balanced and well done. He was a great source and I was grateful that he was a part of the code talker story.

TOM RANDANT

Tom Randant was a real character, had a marvelous sense of humor, and was most willing to share his memories about the war. He was a communications instructor teaching Morse code and his encounters with the code talkers were hilarious. He became a valuable resource and we corresponded on a regular basis. The one story he gave me that I didn't include in the book dealt with "Raisin Jack," the making of alcohol in combat zones. It had other names like "Torpedo Juice," "Jungle Hooch," and "Kick-a-poi-joy Juice" to name a few. According to Marine Corps rules, this was strictly forbidden, so of course it was the one they violated first and often.

"War," he said "is just about the most useless occupation any human can think to participate in, but if you're going to make young men fight and kill other humans, you should allow them a taste of something that will give them nightmare-free sleep. Besides, the water available was not the best or the freshest, in fact, it often resembled the smell of the latrines.

"The recipes were simple: ferment any and all available fruit in a container that could be sealed, add grain alcohol, and let it sit for a couple of days. The oppressive heat made it a dicey process and you couldn't let it sit unattended for too long. Many times those containers blew sky high, and we'd have to start all over again. The Navajos were the best at foraging for fruit and they seemed to have a knack for brewing. Knowing that alcohol was not legal on their reservation, I often wondered where they learned this particular skill.

"I always made sure that duty came first and the brew second, and no one under my command ever broke those rules. I always made sure no one drank themselves unconscious. Hangovers could get you and a whole lot of others killed."

R. G. ROSENQUIST

R. G. Rosenquist, a former member of the Raider Battalions, was the historian for the Raider Museum in Virginia, and he provided the names of the eighteen Navajo code talkers who served among the four Raider Battalions. He wasn't willing to share any recollections with me, but his information was valuable nonetheless. He invited me to attend the Raider Battalion reunion in 1994 to be held in Las Vegas and I couldn't refuse. During the banquet I presented the Commandant of the Marine Corps with an autographed copy of *Navajo Weapon* and I received a copy of the history of the Raiders, *Our Kind of War,* in return. Sadly, I never received any responses from any members of the Raiders who were willing to share information about the code talkers and the role they played within them.

But by now, I had such good information that all I needed to do was blend it in with documents and the code talker recollections, and their story would begin to take shape. The more difficult thing to accomplish would be getting the code talkers to agree to not only meet with me, but talk to me. I didn't know exactly how difficult that was going to be, but I was about to find out.

CHAPTER 8

THE CODE TALKERS SPEAK, PART 1

I'D MADE PLANS TO BE IN GALLUP during the Inter-Tribal Indian Ceremonial because Mary thought it would give me the greatest access to the most code talkers. I'd sent letters requesting meetings with the following men, who agreed to meet with me: Wilsie Bitsie, Kee Etsicitty, Bill Toledo, Sam Billison, Harold Foster, Teddy Draper, and Paul Blatchford. I had a three-inch three-ring binder full of documents to show them and a list of questions for each man. I purchased a battery-operated tape recorder, a twelve-pack of blank cassettes, extra batteries, and two legal size tablets, and made sure I had good, workable pens.

Mom and Melinda were going with me and I wanted to try to experience as much of the ceremonial as time permitted. Mary told me that her oldest grandson Michael would be performing in one of the evening's competitions and we were all looking forward to seeing that. I asked Mary if there was something I could use to impress upon the men how important it was to talk with me about their experiences, and she gave me the following information.

"If they seem to be reluctant to answer your questions about the code or what they did with it in combat, remind them how they learned about their culture from their elders." She gave me a series of questions to ask them which I thought were absolutely brilliant. It was also kind of a clever way to guilt them into revealing their information and I didn't hesitate to consider using it. As you will see, it became the one "trigger" that opened them up and that ultimately filled my cassettes with information.

BERT TALLSALT

Walking around the grounds of the Red Rock Arena, viewing the varied displays of Native American art, sculptures, dream catchers, and so many other things was almost overwhelming. I spotted a tall Navajo in a Navajo Code Talkers Association uniform and approached him.

"Excuse me, sir. May I ask you a couple of questions?"

He smiled and said, "Yes."

I began, "I see by your insignia that you served in the Fourth Marine Division. I would like to interview you for a book I'm writing about the code talkers."

"What is your name?" he asked.

"Sally McClain," I replied.

Before I could say anything else, Carl appeared, came over and began speaking with Bert in Navajo and the exchange was fascinating to watch. When they were done, Carl smiled, winked at me, and left.

"You have a very important friend," Bert said.

"Yes, Carl has been very helpful in arranging interviews with fellow code talkers," I said.

"I'm hungry," he said. "You can ask me questions while I eat."

We walked to the food court area where Bert ordered a bowl of mutton stew and a fresh piece of fry bread. As he reached into his pocket I said, "Lunch is my treat." I ordered a piece of fry bread and drizzled honey all over it.

We sat at a picnic table as drums were throbbing in the background. I took out my tablet because trying to use the tape recorder would be futile with all the background noise surrounding us. "How is your stew?" I asked.

He smiled and said, "Just like my grandmother used to make. Sheep are very important to the Navajo people. They give us their wool and their meat. As a boy, I was responsible for taking care of the sheep. If I didn't do it the right way, my grandmother would scold me in a way that made sure I did it right the next time."

I smiled and said, "Yes, I've heard that about Navajo grandmothers. One of the code talkers told me that his grandmother would have made a good drill sergeant."

He laughed and agreed with that statement. When he was finished, I took out a pen and prepared to write down whatever he was willing to tell me.

"How did you learn about the Marine Corps's need for Navajo recruits?" I asked.

"Well," he began, "I was in school at Kayenta and it was near the end of the first term at high school, I think in 1943, when a Navajo boy showed up and gave us a lecture about the Marine Corps. I think his name was John Benally. He told us that the Corps was the best fighting force in the world. He looked real sharp in that uniform, and I was ready to join on the spot.

"He told us that if we got through boot camp we would be assigned to special duty, duty that only Navajos could do. That made me even more ready to join up. He said we had to be eighteen years old to enlist, or if we were seventeen, we had to have a parent give permission. He told us where the nearest recruiting office was and said to think real hard about what we wanted to do.

"I just turned sixteen, and I didn't want to wait another year to join the fight. I took the papers from Mr. Benally and went back to my dorm room. I was too far away from home to go there, get permission, and get back in time to go to the recruiting office. Then I had an idea. There was a Chapter House not far from the school, and I knew that if I told an elder my story, he would sign the papers and I could join the Marines the next week.

"I walked to the Chapter House the next day, spotted an elder, and told him what I needed from him. At first he looked at me like I was a little crazy, but I explained that joining the Marines was what I wanted to do. We sat at a table, I pulled out the papers, and he asked what he needed to do. I told him I need him to print his name where the section said 'parent.' He told me he didn't know how to write his name. I was crushed. I had walked a long way to get this done and now it seemed I was going to have to wait a whole year before I could join.

"I looked again at the parent section and saw that there was another way to do this. It said either a name or a thumbprint was required. I got excited and told the elder he could use his thumbprint instead of his name. He got up and walked to a desk and pulled out a small bottle of ink. He put a small drop on a piece of paper, swirled it around in a circle, then put his thumb in it. He pressed it to the paper to make sure it didn't blur, then walked back and put it in the section I indicated. I was so happy!

"I thanked him for his help, he wished me good luck, and I went back to my dorm. I tucked the papers under my pillow that night and couldn't wait for Monday to come. I went to the recruiting office early Monday morning, gave them the papers, and was sworn into the Marine Corps before lunch."

"That is amazing," I said. "To think you went to that extreme to join the Marine Corps."

"We knew that the war was important and anyone who could contribute to winning it is what we did," Bert replied.

"What was boot camp like for you? Were you in a mixed platoon?" I asked.

"Yes, I was with five other Navajo boys. We talked late in the night about where we were from, what clan we belonged to, and where we went to school," he replied. "Boot camp wasn't too hard, the drills made you think like one person, and the food was better than what I got at the boarding school."

"What did you think about the code school?" I asked.

"I was surprised. Using my language to defeat the enemy was a real smart thing to do. I felt important. The drills and tests were hard at first, but as I learned more words, it made a lot more sense and I knew that no enemy would ever figure out what we were saying."

"Being assigned to the 4th Marine Division, you served on Iwo Jima?" I asked.

He became very somber at the mention of that island. I felt he was probably going to struggle with that experience and wasn't sure what, if anything, he was prepared to tell me.

He sighed and said, "Iwo was a really bad place. There was nothing on that rock that was green. I'd never been anywhere where something didn't grow, but Iwo looked evil, smelled evil, and was evil. There was so much death there, so many friends died, and all I could do was keep sending messages to kill the Japs.

"After the war I came home, got married, and had twelve children. I tried to forget about the war and didn't tell anyone how I used my language. I joined the Association a couple of years ago, and it's been good to talk with other code talkers who lived through what I did."

I sensed that I wasn't going to be able to ask any specific questions and that this interview was pretty much over.

"I want to thank you for the service you performed during the war, and I appreciate the sacrifice you made to keep this country free," I said.

He smiled, shook my hand, and walked away. I sat there for a long time thinking about what he'd revealed to me. I was stunned by the lengths he went to in order to join the war effort, especially for a country that historically had not treated his people all that fairly. I packed up my tablet, searched for Mom and Melinda, and was determined to enjoy the rest of the ceremonial.

The following day, I would spend almost six hours with a code talker who gave me huge amounts of vital information about the code, their duties, and an encounter with a Raider Battalion that makes me laugh to this day.

KEE ETSICITTY

Kee Etsicitty lives just outside of Gallup in Vanderwagen and works as a Navajo rodeo announcer. He served in the 3rd Marine Division on Bougainville, Guam and Iwo Jima, was a member of the second all-Navajo platoon and was at first a little reluctant to talk about the code. He said, "He, along with all the code talkers of the 3rd Division were told in no uncertain terms to not talk about what they had done during the war. Don't tell your parents, girlfriend, brothers, or sisters. In fact, it would be best to forget what you did during the war," he stated." Kee complied to the nth degree and returned home and never told anyone what he did during the war.

I began to build a connection with him by asking him about boot camp. It always seemed to be a good place to start and it wasn't a secret. He also gave me permission to record him.

"Boot camp wasn't too rough," he began, "but washing clothes was something none of us Navajos had ever done. The women always did this chore, while the men were responsible for taking care of the sheep, goats, and cattle. The drill sergeant would come by and inspect the clothes we put on the line to dry, and would rip them off when they dripped too much. He'd make us wring and wring them until there was no water left to wring out. He'd say, 'You think your momma will be in a combat zone to wash and dry your clothes? Well, she won't, so you'll need to wash your own clothes so get to it!' He was strict, but wringing out the clothes developed some arm strength I didn't have before, so I guess he knew what he was doing.

"On the rifle range, we were real good at hitting the bull's-eye and I made Expert. Most of the Navajos did real well too. The drills were hard at first, but once we got used to them, we did real well."

He paused, as if he was struggling to think of what to tell me next so I asked him about the code school. He furrowed his brow and I knew he was wondering just exactly what he could tell me. I opened up the binder and began showing him copies of documents and the dictionary and said, "Do you see this stamp on the dictionary?" He nodded his head. "That stamp means that your code has been declassified. It's now okay to talk about it and you won't get in trouble for it." I handed him the pages of the dictionary and he looked through them for what seemed like a long time. "Did you find it difficult to learn and memorize all these terms?" I asked.

He smiled and said, "This was hard, but seeing the things that matched the military word made sense after a while. We'd start real early in the morning and go until about six o'clock at night. The instructors drilled us on pronunciation—the word had to be said right and it had to be memorized. Testing day was always on Fridays and if you didn't get a seventy-five percent you had to take the test over on Saturday. I learned words I never heard of before and learning how to write a military message was difficult. But, we studied at night with each other and passed the final exam. Then I was assigned to the 3rd Marine Division.

"I felt protected going to war using my language. I didn't know what it would do to the enemy, but I was ready to do my best. My first combat action was on Bougainville and the first couple of days I was pretty scared. I sent messages for artillery strikes in code and we hit the spot right where the enemy was hiding. My commanding officer was glad he had us and the rest of the action was just like that, fast and furious."

"Were you aware that you had a bodyguard assigned to protect you and the other code talkers?" I asked.

He frowned, thinking hard and said, "No, but that doesn't mean we didn't have one. We were never allowed to venture out without an armed point man and my commanding officer issued us a side arm with the instruction to 'save the last bullet for yourself.'" *That's interesting.*

We spent the next hour talking about the other campaigns he served in and how he used the code, and then he remembered an incident that happened on Bougainville near the end of the battle.

"We were in a secured area, and one of my buddies noticed there were wild goats on a hill not too far away. Seeing them was like being home so we asked our officer if we could take a point man and hunt the goats. He gave us permission and we ended up killing a couple of small ones. We brought them back, prepared a fire, and put them on a spit. Fresh meat in a combat area is hard to come by and the smell was mouth watering. It must have carried a long way because pretty soon a company of Raiders arrived and asked what we were cooking. One of my buddies said "kids" and they didn't stay long. I think they thought we were cooking children, not baby goats."

We were both laughing. I can only imagine what those Raiders thought about cooking "kids." The Navajos had developed a certain mystique within the Corps, that they were the toughest alive, and I'm sure this is what gave the Raider company pause. The three hours we spent together were filled with great information and Kee managed to answer all my questions. His recollections of Iwo were more of a personal nature, rather than code related, but they were interesting and helpful.

"Was it strange being so far away from home?" I asked.

He sat there for a few moments before answering. "Yes, I'd never seen the ocean and it seemed so big and went on forever. The transport ships were really big and it was hard to see how they could float and not sink into the water. Once we got into combat, everything happened so fast—you didn't have too much time to be afraid. You did your job just like the rest of the Marines and hoped for the best.

"The jungles on Bougainville and Guam were really strange. They were filled with monkeys and strange-colored birds, and the trees often shut out the sky. It was strange to be so far away from home, but then everybody was far from home. I learned to love mangos; I still eat them to this day." He smiled at this recollection and then asked me if I had any other questions for him.

I glanced over my list and said, "I can't think of any at this moment, but if I do, can I write you?"

"Sure," he replied. I packed up the tapes, recorder and notes, shook his hand and thanked him for his time. I also encouraged him to tell his children what he experienced during the war. "It's not just a piece of American history, it's a piece of Navajo history as well. Your children deserve to know how their language was used—they would be very proud of you," I said. He walked me out to my car and I made my way back to Gallup filled with a sense of accomplishment. This interview had gone better than I imagined and Kee gave me some wonderful information about three battles, so I hoped the next code talker would be as open as he had been.

BILL TOLEDO

Bill Toledo lives in Laguna, New Mexico, just about twenty miles west of Albuquerque. His wife is a member of the Laguna tribe, so that is where he resides. Having already spoken with Richard Bonham, I was anxious to hear Bill's side of the story. He began by telling me about his ancestors' Long Walk, his childhood, and the sweat lodge ceremony his grandfather introduced him to.

"My parents died when I was a baby, so I was raised by my grandparents. We always woke up just before dawn, went outside the hogan, said our prayer as Father Sun rose. It was a traditional way of life, prayer in the morning, entering the Hogan and turning to the left, saying a prayer as a sheep was slaughtered, thanking it for the meat and sacrifice it gave to us. Attending the Blessing Way Ceremonies was a real treat. That is like a general dance, a chance to meet other clans and be social with yours. From the time I was four I was responsible for

Sally McClain and Bill Toledo, Colorado Springs, Colorado, 2002.

taking the sheep out to graze every morning. I would sit and look at the far horizon and wonder what lay beyond it."

"Tell me about the Long Walk," I asked.

He closed his eyes for a moment then began the story. "The Long Walk was a time when the white government said the Navajos were making too much trouble and the army came and removed the people from the Four Sacred Mountains to Fort Sumner. Some Navajos hid in Canyon de Chelly, thinking they were safe there. The army starved them until they surrendered. They didn't allow them to take extra food. Most walked behind the few wagons there were. If someone fell behind, the soldiers would shoot them. They only stopped to rest at night and many went hungry and thirsty.

"Many young children and old ones died, but the parents weren't allowed to bury them. If anyone died, they were just left where they fell. When they got to Bosque Redondo, the land was hard and you couldn't plant anything. The water was full of alkaline, not good to drink for the People or animals. The People lived on white men's flour and bad beef. No wood to build hogans, so they dug into the ground away from the heat and cold. The People believed the Holy People were punishing them for leaving the Four Sacred Mountains.

"Years went by, and then a peace commission came to see how bad the Navajos were and decided to let them go back home. Many of the Head Men stated their case for returning, promising not to make any trouble if they would just let them return. The commission finally agreed, and after four years of hard suffering, the People were allowed to go back to the land of our ancestors."

I was choking back tears at this recital. Bill spoke as if he had been one of those who had endured such misery. I would learn that the rest of the code talkers I interviewed spoke in the same manner when telling this story. To change the subject, I asked him where he went to school.

"Then when I was six, a man from the BIA came and took me and my cousin Preston off to boarding school. I was real scared, the teachers were mean, wouldn't let us speak our language. They would give us extra detention, kitchen duty, and even wash our mouths with brown soap if we got caught doing it."

It took a great deal of restraint to keep from saying anything about this inhuman treatment. I was incensed that they were treated in this manner and were allowed to get away with it. He continued his story.

"I did real good in school, learned to speak English, but couldn't wait to get home. The summers were filled with chores my grandmother assigned me and it didn't last long enough. Then, when I was in my last year of school, Johnny Manuelito came and spoke with us about joining the Marines. Boy, he looked so sharp in that uniform, spoke about how we could make a difference in the war effort and I joined after I graduated. I was assigned to the 297th Platoon that was all Navajos, and we went through boot camp. The drills and discipline were hard, but we all did real well. I was assigned to the 3rd Marine Division and our first combat was on Bougainville."

He spoke about ending up lost and marched at gunpoint to his commanding officer. "Richard was assigned to me and we spent a lot of time talking about our homes, how we lived and other normal talk. We became best friends. I didn't learn that he was my bodyguard until after the war was over. Somehow we lost touch with each other and didn't meet again until 1980. Now we meet each year with the other members of the 27th Regiment and I feel real good about those men I served with. I finally learned what was beyond that far horizon."

He told me how difficult it was to learn the code. Test day was the hardest, but he knew that what they would do with the code in combat would help end the war. He related his experiences on Guam and Iwo Jima and then what he did once he got home.

"I met my wife and we married and I moved to Laguna and we had our children. I worked at a power plant. It was a hard job to get because the man in charge heard that Navajos were lazy and unreliable, so I didn't tell him I was a Navajo, I was Laguna when I applied. After a while, he figured it out and said he was wrong, that I was a good worker and he wouldn't be afraid to hire more Navajos. That made me feel good. I set a good example and a lot of other Navajos ended up working at the power plant with me." We spent more than three hours going over everything he wanted to reveal to me. I was thrilled with his cooperation and his substance. He had given me a great deal to work with on three important Marine Corps battles, and he was easy to speak with.

"Can you explain to me how you could want to serve and protect a country that treated you so harshly as a child?" I asked.

He was quiet for a few moments before he replied. "We are taught from a very young age that the earth is our mother. It gives us food, water, and life. You protect that with your life, no matter what. Navajo land is part of America and if you attack one, you attack the other. There was never a doubt we would do anything to protect our way of life."

I thanked him for his time and said I would be in touch with him. On the drive back to Gallup, my mind raced with all he had told me. I was still boiling inside over the treatment he and other Navajo children were subjected to in that government-run boarding school. I could not imagine letting my child ever be treated in that manner.

Where did our government get the notion that forced acculturation was permissible in any way, shape, or form? Why was it "acceptable" to inflict this on Native Americans? Then I remembered seeing a photograph of a sign in one of the books about the Navajos that said: "Tradition, the Enemy of Progress." What Neanderthal came up with that? Deep down inside I knew there would never be an explanation that would make what happened acceptable to me.

That evening, Mom, Melinda, and I attended the evening dance performance at Red Rock Arena and it was an incredible experience. The dancing, drums, singing, and costumes were fabulous. Even though I only have about a 64th degree of Choctaw and Cherokee blood, I felt a real kinship with all the dancers. The group of Aztec dancers were the most exotic and it felt as if I had stepped back in time, watching an ancient ceremonial. It was a wonderful conclusion to what had been a wonderful day. I was really looking forward to my next two interviews with Harold Foster and Sam Billison.

SAM BILLISON

Sam Billison was really tall—a surprise to me because most Navajos are somewhere in the 5'6" to 5'8" range and he was close to 6'1". He told me in a proud voice that he was the only Navajo that had a PhD in Education. As we began the interview, he started with the story of the Long Walk and then his boot camp experience.

"In boot camp, you have to be able to swim four lengths of the pool before you graduate. Growing up, we didn't have swimming pools, only small creeks and ponds that weren't very deep, so I learned to dog paddle. I thought that was swimming until boot camp. The instructor told us to jump in and start swimming. I started dog paddling and got halfway before I sank to the bottom. My feet touched and I pushed myself back up, paddled about a foot, went down, came back up, paddled a foot, and went down again. The rule was if a man went down for a third time, someone jumped in and brought them up. The instructor said, 'Chief, I thought you told me you knew how to swim!' I said, 'I thought I did.'"

We were both laughing at this recollection. "Then the instructor told me to report one hour each morning before breakfast and he would teach me how to pass the swim test. When I did, I was happy to see that I wasn't the only recruit who didn't know how to swim. The rest of boot camp went real well, and right before graduation, a sergeant came up to me and asked if I was an Indian. I told him no, I was a Navajo. He got a little irritated but told me to report to the communication office; I would be given special duty. So, after graduation I went to the communication office and was put in the code school the following week. The instructors told us that what we did in the school was "Secret" and we were never to talk about it or write home about it. If we did, we would end up in the brig. Testing day was every Friday and you had to pass the final exam with 75 percent or better to qualify as a code talker.

"The lessons were hard. Learning all those terms and how to use them in a message was worse than anything I learned in the boarding school, but seeing how we were using our language for combat made me feel proud. Everyone was doing something for the war effort: gathering scrap metal, rationing food, shoes, and tires, so using my language was another contribution. When I graduated code school, I was assigned to the 5th Marine Division and shipped out to Hawaii. Training

Sam Billison, Gallup, New Mexico, 1994.

for the next mission, us code talkers spent a lot of time in the field with radios practicing sending messages.

"We boarded transport ships and set out, didn't know where we were going until three nights before debarkation. I was assigned to go with a reconnaissance patrol to report on beach conditions and send the information back to the ship in code. That was a scary trip. The Japs opened fire when they spotted us and we were lucky to make it back alive. Iwo was a bad place, lots of friends died there … I was lucky to be on board a communication ship for the worst of the fighting.

"After the war was over, I came home and took my GI Bill benefits and went back to school. I wanted to improve the schools on the reservation, taught for a lot of years, and then was appointed to the school board of the Navajo Nation. I also wanted our children to be able to speak Navajo without punishment. I wanted them to learn it from an early age and speak it fluently like I did. That's what I learned from the war. Our language had a purpose. It saved lives. It had value."

"Was it strange being so far from home?" I asked.

"Yes," he replied. "The world outside of the Navajo Nation is a strange and sometimes dangerous place. I had my language to protect me and I was thankful. When I went away to higher education, I didn't have a hard time adjusting to that world. The Marine Corps taught me that. They taught me that I could succeed at anything if I worked hard enough at it. I'm proud to be a Navajo and a Marine. Do you have any more questions for me?"

At the moment, I couldn't think of any, so I thanked him for his time and told him I would be in touch. My appointment with Harold was in about twenty minutes and I needed to prepare for it.

HAROLD FOSTER

Sam left just as Harold arrived. They conversed in Navajo for a few minutes and then Harold sat down and asked if I was enjoying the ceremonial.

"Yes," I replied. "The dancing, artwork, and food have been a really nice experience. I'm afraid I have become addicted to fry bread."

He smiled and said, "Do you know the story of fry bread?" "No," I said.

"Fry bread came about after the removal of the Navajo from the Four Sacred Mountains," he stated. "Since our ancestors couldn't grow corn at Bosque Redondo they had to live off white man's flour. The women would mix the flour with water and use lard to fry it because they didn't have a proper oven to bake the bread. They have been using it ever since … a reminder of that imprisonment … a reminder to never let it happen again. It's really good with a drizzle of honey."

"Oh, it's a slice of ambrosia with honey," I said.

He smiled and said, "What else do you need me to tell you about the war?"

"Anything that you feel will be helpful in explaining how the code was used," I replied.

"Well, on Iwo, because the Japs were buried underground, precise artillery strikes were the only way to defeat them. The messages I sent dealt with those situations. The worst was near Kitano Point, near the end of the battle, Japs didn't want to surrender. We had to use gasoline to burn them out."

I could tell by the look on his face that this was a very painful memory. I wanted to reach out and remove the pain he was experiencing, erase the sight and sound of those incidents. But that kind of power I do not have. After a long pause, he continued.

"When it was over, we finally got the chance to shower and shave. I don't know how long it had been since my last one and it took quite a while to clean all the grime off. That shower acted like a cleansing ceremony and I felt a lot better after that. When I came home, I started working for the Navajo Health Division, serving as an interpreter for the doctors and nurses, so using my language this time was for healing, not killing. Anything else?"

"I can't think of anything, but I want to thank you for your service during the war. What you and everyone else who served did allows me and many generations to have a life of freedom and choices and I appreciate your sacrifice." He smiled, shook my hand, and left. My head was swimming with all I had learned so far. From my research, I knew the South Pacific campaigns were brutal, but until you have a veteran sitting in front of you recalling that brutality, it's easy to dismiss. I would never dismiss it again.

We only had one day left, so it was decided that we would just enjoy the last day of the ceremonial. Walking through the crowds, I ran into Teddy Draper, Paul Blatchford, and Wilsie Bitsie, and arranged to interview them at a later time. I also knew that there was more documentation waiting for me to discover in the archives, information necessary to tie all the bits and pieces together. All in all, it had been a fabulous five days and the trip home was filled with those remembrances.

I spent the next couple of months transcribing the interviews, marking certain passages and cross-referencing them with the applicable campaign. I felt like a weaver working on an enormous, complicated tapestry, tying threads of storylines to blend with the whole. I began to see the purpose behind the code—the validity of how it was used and why.

I called Mary a few days after my return and shared with her all that I had gleaned in the interviews. Then she gave me a piece of information that startled me. "Back in 1970," she said, "Doris Duke donated grant money to the University of Utah to interview and record the code talkers. I think they managed to interview between fifty or sixty men, a lot of whom have passed away, a number of 'The First 29' included. You might want to contact them and see if you can get copies of those interviews to fill in the blanks."

"That's amazing," I said. "Right now, I don't have enough code talkers from all the divisions, so it is definitely worth a letter or phone call. Thanks for the info." *Code talkers were interviewed back in 1970? I wonder what they revealed.* I had other things to do before contacting the University, so I put it on a list of things to do. The rest of the year was spent working on tying all the information together and trying to get a feel for how the story should be laid out. Integrating the code talkers into the battles was going to be difficult, but the only way to show how much their code was valued and used was to do it this way.

I made plans to return to Washington, D.C. in late March to finish obtaining every bit of documentation I could get my hands on. Then I would make one more trip back to the rez and finish interviewing the remaining code talkers. Between work, Melinda, and the book I was stretched pretty thin, but the anticipation of learning the true and complete code talker story fueled me in ways that made my hectic life somewhat manageable.

CHAPTER 9

EXTENDED RESEARCH

IN MARCH OF 1991 I RETURNED TO THE WASHINGTON, D.C. area and made a beeline for Suitland. I'd also made plans to spend a day and night with Henry and Alice. I was anxious to meet them in person, and the drive to their house would be a chance to see some of Virginia.

So far, there had been some strange twists and turns on this journey and there were more waiting for me in Suitland. Checking in with an archivist, I was informed that a rather large record group had been located that dealt with Iwo Jima. It hadn't been sorted or catalogued yet, but I was welcome to search the twenty boxes and copy what I found useful.

Wahoooo! I just struck the mother lode of all time! I asked the archivist when I could get access. She replied the first five boxes would be in a separate research room in about an hour. I went down the hall, stowed my purse in a locker, and got out a blank legal pad, three pens, and money for the copying fees. I would soon be looking at material that possibly hadn't been seen since 1945, and I was both excited and anxious. Iwo was one of the bloodiest and deadliest battles of the South Pacific campaigns. The code talkers had intimated that they played a major role in the conquest of that island, and I hoped that I could find piles of documents of their involvement.

BOX 1

Opening the first box, I saw a jumble of paper. It looked as if the contents had shifted quite a bit over the years and I had to be very careful pulling out the first pile. I emptied the box, placed all the contents on the table in six stacks and began going through each piece of paper. The first few documents were general correspondence dealing with material supply requests, casualty lists, and replacement requests. As I sorted down, I found a CT (Combat Team) 28 radio call log and knew in an instant that some of the messages had been marked for a code talker to send. The code talkers told me that when they were needed to send or receive a message, the call sign "Arizona" or "New Mexico" would precede it. All through this log were those two call signs, and although the messages were in English, I knew that they would have been translated into code before being sent.

My hands were shaking a little. I was actually reading a combat message a code talker would have sent. Then a little chill went through me because the majority of the messages were casualty reports and artillery strike requests. The death toll was devastating and the artillery requests were urgent. I set the log aside to be copied and hoped I could find a code talker that served in the 28th to confirm it.

The rest of the first stack didn't have anything relating to the code talkers. I went through the second and about halfway through, I found a grid map of the island. Grid maps were used to pinpoint enemy positions to coordinate mortar, artillery, and strafing attacks. I set it aside to copy and continued, ultimately finding about twenty documents referring to the code talkers. I carefully re-stacked the documents back in the box and opened the second box. The majority of the contents of this box consisted of beach consolidation reports, grave registrations, and general operations orders.

The third, fourth, and fifth boxes held nothing relating to the code talkers, but it was fascinating reading nonetheless. As disturbing as it was, the dissection of this battle helped me understand what was taking place. Then I came across a list of pre-debarkation material lists and it stopped me cold. Among the items listed were six thousand wooden crosses. This was the true price of war. It just doesn't cross the minds of everyday people to think about going to war and ordering crosses to mark the graves of the fallen. I certainly never had that thought and it made me wonder if this list had been published in the papers throughout America, what the public's reaction would have been.

On my way to lunch, I told the archivist I was finished with the first five boxes and was ready for the next batch. She assured me I would have access to the next five after I returned. The fresh air felt so good. Digging though those dusty boxes and having to examine the death and destruction of so many human beings was exhausting. I took a rather long lunch, wanting to clear my head and prepare myself for the remainder of the record group.

Over the next two days, I sorted through thousands of documents, copying well over two hundred. By the end, I was drained by all I had learned about Iwo Jima. I wanted nothing more than to go through different record groups to find lighter sources regarding the code talkers. During the last two days I spent at Suitland, I managed to find another two hundred and fifty documents, and felt I had examined every available group and obtained the military proof I needed. Hopefully, with everything in hand, I would be able to weave the code talker story into a sensible, logical, realistic revelation of their unique service.

After this emotional and exhausting research, I was ready for Henry and Alice's hospitality. I drove through some really beautiful country on the way to their house. I arrived just in time for dinner. We greeted each other warmly and said how good it was to finally put faces to the voices. The yard was set up with a table and Henry was grilling meat, so I helped Alice set the table. She'd prepared fresh vegetables from her garden and we talked about Colorado while plating the food. During the meal, we spoke about general things. I told them that when I was growing up, we grew a lot of our own food, and had chickens and pigs, "so I appreciate the taste of fresh produce." I said. "The steak is cooked perfectly, Henry."

"We eat a lot of our meals outdoors when the weather is good," said Henry. "Alice is a real good cook, but I'm the 'Steak Master' in the family. Our children often come over on the weekends and we cook up a mess of food. How old is your daughter?" he asked.

"Melinda will be ten years old in September," I replied.

We spent the rest of the evening talking about camping trips they'd taken to visit Teddy Draper. Henry gave me a tour of his house and upstairs he had an impressive collection of fossils and spent bullets from Civil War battlefields. "This is the one I want to show you. I took this off a dead Jap on Iwo," he said. He handed me a samurai sword and I felt a chill go through me. I was holding an actual sword from a Japanese commander and despite the fact that it was taken from a dead man, it was a beautiful sword. I asked him where and why he took it.

"Souvenir hunting could get you killed. The Japs would booby trap their dead, if you touched or tried to take anything you could get blown up. I found this a few feet from a dead Jap … didn't look dangerous so I took it. He didn't need it anymore and someday I wanted to show my children who we fought against," he said. I really didn't know what to say. It was clear that Henry still carried a deep enmity for the Japanese, so I steered the conversation in the direction of the Civil

War souvenirs. "Alice and I go metal detecting all around Virginia … found these bullets and some other things like jewelry. I want you to take a couple of the bullets for Melinda. She could find them useful if she does a book report, and I found this shark spine fossil near the beach. Take them with you," he said.

I thanked him for the presents for Melinda and the tour of his collection. We retired for the night, but I had a hard time finding peaceful sleep. I kept seeing a dead Japanese soldier lying covered in blood and Henry carefully extracting his samurai sword. Ah, the spoils of war. I'll never understand why soldiers are so drawn to them. I would never want anything that belonged to an enemy.

Breakfast was wonderful and the time I'd spent with them was, for the most part, a real delight. "Thank you for your hospitality. Staying in hotels during these trips gets real old. It was a real pleasure to have a home-cooked meal. If you ever find yourselves wanting to visit Colorado, you'll have to let me return the hospitality," I said. The drive back to D.C. seemed longer than the one out and I suspect it had to do with the fact that holding that Japanese sword unnerved me. Henry and Alice were wonderful people and the stories Henry told me about Teddy Draper and James Cohoe would be of great value to the code talker story, but I was more than ready to go home.

The next two months was a process of sorting and matching the documents in chronological order, highlighting with different colors pertinent paragraphs that would be used for each battle. Mary was right—at times most of these documents raised more questions than answers. I knew I would have to find a reliable Marine Corps resource to make sense of some of the orders issued regarding the code talkers.

UNIVERSITY OF UTAH

Summer was fast approaching and I needed to make another trip to the rez and finish interviewing as many code talkers as possible. I also wanted to search the Doris Duke Collection of recorded interviews and see what could be gleaned there. I sent them a letter requesting a list of code talkers on record and asked if copying them was a possibility. They replied that there were sixty voice and transcript recordings and I would be allowed to copy only thirty per request. Picking out thirty might be difficult but I would make my decision after I saw what was in them.

In August, Melinda was going to spend two weeks in Utah with her father and this would give me the perfect opportunity. This trip would also coincide with the Gallup Inter-Tribal Indian Ceremonial, so I would have access to the code talkers I missed the year before. I sent off requests for interviews with Wilsie Bitsie, Paul Blatchford, and Teddy Draper. They all replied they would interview with me at the appointed times and I was really looking forward to this, my last research trip to the rez.

Melinda and I drove to Utah. I dropped her off, and the next day headed for the treasures of information I would find at the University. I checked in at the library desk and was shown to a small research room. I was given the list of code talkers and wrote down my first ten requests. I was in a state of anticipation and couldn't wait to learn what the men had revealed back in 1970. I guess I should have braced myself for some disappointment, but even if I had, it wouldn't have done much good.

The first code talker interview consisted of the interviewer asking him about his life before the war. The questions they asked about the war were sophomoric at best. I had to remind myself that the interviewers may not have known the details about the code talkers or what they had done during the war. Still, there were bits and pieces that were valuable, and instead of ordering a complete copy, I simply wrote down what I thought was pertinent. It was, after all, the first opportunity these men had to speak about the war, their experiences, and the code. Many of them were still reluctant to elaborate about the code and how they used it, but it was enlightening nonetheless.

By the end of the day, I had ordered copies of thirty code talkers and felt I finally had enough information to tie in to tell their story. Now it was time to head for Navajo country and complete this stage of the story.

CHAPTER 10

THE CODE TALKERS SPEAK, PART 2

I SPENT THE FIRST DAY MEETING WITH CARL AND MARY, sharing all I had gleaned from the Iwo Jima record group. I also brought them copies of everything I had found to date. "I'm absolutely amazed at what you have found. This is almost unbelievable," Mary said.

"Yeah, now all I have to do is make sense out of all of it and align it with the code talkers' experiences. Piece of cake." I replied.

Mary laughed. "Well it will be a very tasty piece of cake. Who are you meeting with?"

"I have confirmed appointments with Teddy Draper, Paul Blatchford, and Wilsie Bitsie. I can honestly say that having to wade through all that material about Iwo was mentally exhausting. I really don't know how anyone who served on that hellhole managed to survive with any shred of sanity or humanity intact. Iwo gives *me* nightmares and I wasn't even there."

Mary sat in silence then Carl said, "War is not good for the soul. Gotta find a better way of getting along with each other. But our ceremonies give us a way to heal and the rest you just have to find a way to deal with. Little One, you did a good job." I blushed, which is something I rarely do. His "Little One" endearment almost brought tears to my eyes.

"I'm still not sure how this all came to be, but whatever force is at work, I will always be grateful because it allowed me the opportunity to meet the two of you," I said.

"Little One, you may never know the reason, but your life and the code talkers were meant to meet. Don't question it, just go with it. That's why I knew you were the one, you've proved you had the desire to find the truth and I'm proud of you," Carl said.

I managed to choke out, "Thanks. I still haven't found everything to explain certain aspects of the story, but I think I've got enough to inform the public of the scope of the code talkers' service. I'm hoping this last group will fill in certain blanks about the code and Philip Johnston, so as you advise, I'll just go with it."

We spent the rest of the day examining the multitude of documents and found some of them very amusing. I did ask about the meeting with the BIA and the Marine Corps brass. "Mary, why do you think it was necessary that the Marine Corps brass met with the BIA? I've never quite understood that." I said.

"Well, you have to remember the BIA controls just about every aspect of Native Americans' existence. They monitor the health departments, education, agriculture, resources, and tribal lands. They are supposed to be fair, honest guardians and perhaps because of the treaties with the government, the Corps wanted to make sure they had their opinion, and perhaps to see if permission was needed before recruiting the Navajos. I've heard there are some treaties that included clauses that members of a particular tribe could not bear arms either against or for the United States," Mary replied.

"I can't tell you how sick and angry that makes me feel. No other minority anywhere in this country has to endure this level of interference or control. Yeah, I know, they are considered historically 'conquered' people but it is just so … wrong!" I said.

Mary smiled and Carl nodded his head. "Be that as it may, and we could debate this issue forever and a day without resolution, the Corps did what they felt was necessary to clear the way to recruit the Navajos," Mary replied.

"Well, at least the BIA's opinion gave the Corps tacit permission to not only recruit the Navajos, but seemed to feel that using their language was a feasible idea." I said.

"Kind of shoots Philip Johnston's boast of it being his original idea down in flames." Mary said.

"Down in flames and smashed into the ground." I replied. We all laughed.

"Some of the code talkers had a bad Navajo nickname for him. They called him 'itchy butt.' They said he was always walking around scratching his ass, must have had hemorrhoids." Carl said.

"He said he spoke Navajo. Did he ever know what they called him?" I asked.

"He didn't understand as much Navajo as he said he did, so I don't think so." Carl replied.

"The joke was definitely on him!" I said.

Then I asked Mary if she knew anyone who might have known Philip Johnston. "Well," she said, "there is one person who said he knew him … Martin Link. He once told Carl and I that Johnston confessed to him that he had faced a court-martial for some incident involving the code talker program."

"What! Are you serious? Did it have anything to do with the *Arizona Highways* article?" I asked.

Mary smiled, "We suspect so. Martin said he never revealed exactly what led up to the charge, but having read the Marine Corps response to the incident, gives you the idea that that is exactly what happened." I sat there in stunned silence. How could that man have risked the security of the code talkers? I would definitely have to investigate this matter. I just didn't quite know where to start.

We changed the subject and went over more of the documents I'd found. Carl finally agreed to share one particular memory with me that wasn't covered in his autobiography. He related how he had been injured on Saipan, suffered a serious concussion and woke up days later in a hospital in Pearl Harbor. When he finally woke up he found himself in a white room, in a bed with white sheets, and believed he was dead. He looked around the room, noticed flowers in a vase on a bedside table, then slowly turned his head and looked out a window. He knew in that moment he wasn't dead or in heaven because heaven would not have a battleship. It was touching and hilarious the way he related it and I knew the readers would find it amusing.

The evening was drawing near and I needed to head back to Gallup. My meeting with Wilsie was scheduled for nine o'clock the next morning and I wanted to prepare my questions. They wished me luck with the interviews and we agreed to meet in a couple of days. The drive back was so pleasant. Carl and Mary were wonderful people and I was so happy they were involved in this process.

WILSIE BITSIE

I got up early, had breakfast at Nikki's Café, then headed to Wilsie's, hoping he would help tie up loose ends regarding the formation of the code. I remembered that both Eugene and Carl said he had the best boot camp stories and the clearest

Wilsie Bitsie, Gallup, New Mexico, 1989.

recollection of how the code was created. He would prove to be a treasure trove of exactly what I needed.

I knocked on his door and waited for a few minutes. When he failed to respond, I began to wonder if he had forgotten our appointment and I began to feel disappointed. I knocked again, a little more loudly, and waited for a response. Just as I thought he wasn't home, I turned to leave, and the door opened.

"What do you want?" Wilsie stated.

I turned to face him and said, "I'm Sally McClain. I wrote you about an interview." He said nothing. "Carl … Carl said you had some great stories about boot camp and the code and I'm hoping you will allow me to interview you," I said.

He opened the door and said, "Come in." He sat down in a recliner and watched me like a hawk as I set down my binder, tape recorder, and note pad. I loaded a blank tape and then sat in a chair opposite him. "I've been doing research about the code talkers and plan to write the story of the service you rendered during the South Pacific campaigns. May I have permission to record your experiences?" I asked.

He sat there, staring at me for a few minutes then said, "I have my great-grandfather's Navajo name. He signed the Treaty of 1868."

I didn't know how to reply to that remark so I said, "You must be very proud of that." Another long silence ensued and I began wondering if he was going to cooperate.

"I have some boot camp stories you might like. Yeah, you can record me if you want," he said. For the next thirty minutes, he regaled me with some of the most amusing recollections of his boot camp experiences. The ones about his demerits and the ensuing punishments were hilarious. Especially the time when he had to clean the doghouse and give the camp mascot, a bulldog, a bath. It appeared that he was warming up and opening up and I sat in respectful silence. When it got to the creation of the code he became reluctant to elaborate. This was where I used the tool that Mary gave me to coax the story out of him.

"May I ask you a few questions?"

"Yes," he replied. I cleared my throat and took a deep breath to calm myself.

"Can any Navajo child ask any elder about the Hero Twins?"

"Yes."

"Can any Navajo child ask any elder about Spider Woman?" I asked.

"Yes."

"Okay, can any Navajo child ask any elder about what the code talkers did during the war?" I asked. There was a long pause, he frowned, then started to laugh.

"No," he replied.

"Exactly," I said. "You are the *only* elders that know this piece of Navajo history. So by your own cultural standards, isn't it your duty to make this information available to the entire tribe?"

He looked stunned for a brief moment, then said with a straight face, "Are you sure you're not Navajo?"

I smiled and then proceeded to show him a copy of the combat dictionary with the declassification stamp on it. He looked at it for a long time before replying, "Wow. Where did you find this?"

"In Marine Corps records in the Suitland Branch of the National Archives." I replied.

"This was the hardest thing any of us ever did. I had learned to type in school so the guys made me write down the words we created. They aren't spelled the way we speak them, but I came as close as I could and I guess it worked," he said. "Everything we created was locked up in a safe at the end of the day. I didn't type this version."

I asked him to explain how they arrived at using the word "stutter" for the country of Italy. He laughed and said, "Well, if we'd had a map, we sure would have given it the Navajo name for 'boot' but one of the guys said he went to school with an Italian kid who stuttered, so that's what we used. Crazy, huh!"

"Did you know Philip Johnston?" I asked.

He snarled and said, "That man was crazy! He was crazy! Walked around thinking he could speak our language and he couldn't. Was always scratching his ass, too. I heard later he tried to take credit for our code, but Carl set him straight. I served in the Carlson's Raider Battalion with Eugene."

"Yes, I interviewed Eugene last year and he said you would give me more details about that."

Wilsie spent another forty-five minutes telling me about his time with the Raiders, the last patrol on Guadalcanal, and finding his friend on Guam and believing him to be dead. He mentioned a couple of commanders, and I opened my notebook and found a couple of documents with their signatures and handed them to him. He read them with a fond look on his face and proceeded to tell me about what the letters referred to.

"I knew Ira Hayes … he asked me why did he survive, when so many others died? Why was he the one the commanding officer called to help raise that flag on Iwo? Why was it him instead of me? He hated the spotlight the Corps put him in. He told me he knew he wouldn't live to be an old man and when they murdered him, I cried for days."

Murdered? I don't recall any reference to Ira being murdered. All the information about him said he died a drunk—froze to death. "I'm sorry, but I thought Ira froze to death, drunk?"

Wilsie snorted. "Yeah, he froze to death after the guys who robbed him hit him in the head and dumped him down a ravine. He'd been gambling with his brother Kenny and won a shitload of money from some white guys. Ira'd always been good with cards, loved to gamble. He sent a lot of money home to his mother during the war, money he won at cards and dice. Ira was tortured by the death he witnessed, a lot of veterans drank, a lot of veterans had problems after the war ... still do. All he ever wanted to be was a Marine and when they put him on display, took him away from his unit, he didn't do real well. He was embarrassed by the attention when that statue was unveiled; he tried to tell the press that the real heroes were the ones who didn't make it home. They didn't listen, thought he was just another drunk Indian."

There was another long silence. Wilsie was reliving those painful memories and I didn't try to ask any questions. I knew that whatever else he wanted to tell me, he would when he felt like it. I didn't have to wait too long.

"When we were on Guam, the natives came out of hiding, glad to see Americans. They'd been treated real bad by the Japs. Once we secured an area and set up camp and food service the locals came out of hiding. One little boy, Johnny, attached himself to me and three other Raiders. We kind of adopted him, watched out for him when we were off duty, made sure he had something to eat. His family had been killed during the Jap invasion and he had no one to take care of him. When Guam was secured, we took turns taking him with us around the Pacific. He fit into our sea bags and never made a sound. He ended up going to Australia, Saipan, and then back to Guam.

"When orders came through that we had to leave, I told him he couldn't go with me. We found some Red Cross workers and gave him to them; we told him we would write to him and keep in touch with him, send him money for school, money for books and clothes. We all did for a long time. About five years ago a man knocked on my door. I opened it and said, 'What collector agency are you from?' He stood there and asked me if I was Wilsie Bisie. I said yes, then he asked did I fight on Guam, and I said yes. Did I help a young boy named Johnny? I said yes. He was a big man, over six feet, and he bent down and embraced me, lifting me off the ground and said, 'Pappa Wilsie, it's me, Johnny ... Johnny from Guam.'"

I let a tear trickle down my face. This was such a wonderful thing he was sharing with me. "I was speechless. I couldn't believe that the person standing in front of me was the same scrawny, scared little boy of so long ago. He came in and told me that the money we sent enabled him to finish school and then become a teacher. He managed to find all four of us and made a personal appearance to thank us for what we had done for him." Tears were freely falling from Wilsie's eyes. "That was the most wonderful thing that ever happened to me. It made everything we went through during the war worth every minute of it. You just never know where kindness will end up being in return," he said.

"What the four of you did for Johnny was nothing more than what would have been expected of any good, decent human being. You don't ever need to wonder why you joined the fight—Johnny was your answer," I said. He cleared his throat, wiped his eyes, and returned to telling me more about those weeks creating the first code. He said after some engagements, the code talkers would return to Hawaii and learn the new terms other code talkers had created. Practice field drills sharpened the new code words and it was great to see how the code had changed and grown.

"I went back to Pendleton after Guam and instructed in the school. Johnston was always hanging around … looked like he didn't know what to do with himself. Always tried to prove he knew our language when he spoke to us but, he didn't know jack shit. I didn't trust him, didn't like him, didn't want nothing to do with him. He finally got the hint and left us alone," Wilsie stated.

Two hours had passed and I asked if there was anything else he wanted to tell me, combat or personally related. "No, but do you have questions for me?" he asked. I glanced over my list and couldn't think of anything else to ask him.

"No, but if I think of anything may I write to you? Will you answer me back?" I said.

He smiled and assured me he would. "So, you're going to put all this into a book? Am I gonna get a copy?" he asked.

I smiled and said, "Yes, this is all going into a book about the code talkers and you most certainly will receive a copy of the finished product. It's the least I can do for all your assistance. I'm sorry your friend Ira died the way he did. Life really isn't fair, is it?" I said. He didn't reply.

I packed up all my materials and thanked Wilsie once again for his time and for sharing his recollections of the code and his war experiences. The drive back to Gallup was filled with his remembrances running through my head. I still had a lot of unanswered questions about Philip Johnston and I might not find them all, but I was absolutely sure he was not who he claimed to be.

I was really excited to travel to Chinle and interview Teddy Draper and Paul Blatchford. Having spent time with Henry and Alice Hisey, I was anxious to meet with Teddy and hear his side of the story. I was hungry and stopped to eat at the Ranch Kitchen before returning to the motel. I spent the rest of the day organizing Wilsie's interview and prepared questions for the next two code talkers. Sleep that night was peaceful and I awoke refreshed and ready to roll.

TEDDY DRAPER

The drive north from Gallup to Chinle was spectacularly beautiful. I passed green meadows filled with sheep and horses, blue lakes, and sandstone formations that have to be seen to be believed. Words are really inadequate in describing their shapes and colors. Two and a half hours later, I arrived in Chinle, stopped at a gas station, and called Teddy. He gave me directions to his house, which I found rather easily.

I knocked on his door and Teddy welcomed me into his home. I pulled out the tape recorder, pad, pens, and notebook. I asked his permission to record our interview and he agreed.

"What do you want to know?" he asked.

"You can start anywhere you like and reveal to me only what you feel comfortable with. If you are willing, I would like to know about any combat experiences and how you used the code." I said.

He began by telling me about the Long Walk and his childhood. He never saw a white face before the age of fourteen and spoke very little English. He grew up in Canyon del Muerto, a side canyon of Canyon de Chelly, taking care of the flock and living a very Spartan existence. His days were spent outside, obeying his grandmother and helping at shearing time. He was finally rounded up and shipped off to boarding school at fourteen and clearly resented his treatment there

He served as a code talker with CT 28, 5th Marines, and while on Iwo was the one who sent the flag-raising message in code down through the ranks. That gave me goose bumps. I held up my hand, "Excuse me, but did you say you were with Combat Team 28?"

"Yes," he replied.

I went through my notebook and found the message log for CT 28. I handed it to him and asked, "Are any of these messages ones you might have sent in code?"

He looked through all the pages of the log, smiling here and there. "Yeah, I sent a number of them. Give me a pen and I'll mark the ones I sent." He said. I handed him a pen and he spent the next ten minutes marking. This was absolutely thrilling. I could use these in the sections of the battle for Iwo and it would be proof that what they did was crucial to the successful outcome of securing that

Teddy Draper, Washington, D.C., 1995.

island. "You can use the dictionary to turn the messages from English into code. Do you have a copy of it?" he asked.

I pulled it out and showed it to him. He had a rather angry look and said, "This cover is really insulting. I've never seen it. Where did you find it?" he asked.

"In the Marine Corps records in the National Archives. I found it rather offensive myself."

"Yeah, but all the words are there, so you can use it. Who else have you talked with?" he asked.

I told him about my conversations and visits with Henry and Alice, and interviews with the code talkers and veteran Marines.

"Henry and I are real good buddies. They come here every couple of years and we camp out in Canyon de Chelly. We never talk about the war. Bad enough we were in it, don't need to relive it. But we always have a good time and it's good to be with each other," he said.

I spent the next hour listening to Teddy relating his experiences on Iwo Jima. He gave me a lot of technical information. His life after the war was spent painting watercolors of various places on Navajo land, making silver jewelry and selling it in a gallery in Chinle that he and his son, Teddy Junior, own and operate. He stated that "being a Marine was one of the things I'm most proud about. They treated me like everyone else—I was Navajo but never made to feel different. They gave me discipline that's served me all my life. Only thing that upsets me is that none of us ever rose above the rank of sergeant. None of us ever got promotions that other Marines got during or after combat. Came home and the first thing I see is the Marine Corps Marching Band and all of them wore sergeant major stripes on their uniforms."

He was clearly angry and upset at this and then I remembered how the Corps was structured. "I understand how that might have upset you but, what would normally happen to a Marine when he rose in rank?" I asked.

"Well, he would either command a unit or move up nearer the big shots," he replied.

"Exactly. Do you think the Corps could have afforded to lose a code talker due to a promotion? There were only about eighty assigned per division and you weren't a specified unit, no matter how unfair that was, they simply couldn't risk losing a member of a valuable link in their communications." I said.

He sat there for a few moments, digesting what I'd said. "Well, I see your point, but it still stinks," he replied.

"Well, from what I know about Iwo, the whole island stank," I said.

He smiled and said, "You never get that smell out of your nose. Iwo looked like hell, smelled like hell, and was hell. It took me a long time to feel clean after that battle. The Medicine Man gave me an extra cleansing ceremony to make sure the dirt of that place was all gone."

"Did you ever see Philip Johnston at the school?" I asked.

"You mean the man who always scratched his ass?" Teddy replied. We both laughed. "I saw him a couple of times, the instructors said he was a liaison with the brass, but I never saw him in the classroom," Teddy replied.

Two hours had passed and I had to go eat, then get ready for the next code talker interview. I asked him if there was anything else he wanted to talk about, and he said he didn't. I thanked him for his time and said I would be in touch. I drove back to Chinle had a long, relaxing lunch then headed for Paul Blatchford's house. He lived in the opposite direction from Teddy, but I had no trouble finding him.

PAUL BLATCHFORD

Paul Blatchford was a very different code talker. He had a white father and said he never really learned to speak Navajo well. His mother was a Navajo, but she deferred to her husband when it came to teaching the children English over Navajo. Paul had a great sense of humor and the stories he related to me were very amusing. He gave me permission to record him and we spent over two hours in each other's company.

"I originally signed up with the Navy," he began. "Got off the train from Gallup and a Marine recruiter holding a clipboard was calling out names. He passed by me and asked if I was a Navajo and I said 'yes.' He asked me my name, checked his list and said, 'How come I don't have your name?' I told him I signed up with the Navy. 'Hell, what did you do that for? Don't you know the Marines are the best? We have a special place for the Navajos. You need to change your selection. I'll be right back.'

"I didn't know about that, so I waited for him to return. He came back with a Navy recruiter and a piece of paper for me to change services. The Navy guy didn't like his heavy hand, but I figured they would sort it out. I signed the paper he gave me, then the Navy recruiter said it would take a couple of days to sort out and I would still have to go to the Navy Recruit Depot. So, I went off with the other recruits and next day started boot camp.

"Two days later, a Marine showed up with transfer papers and told me I was going with him. There was only one problem—I didn't have my own clothes anymore. When you enter boot camp, they take everything civilian from you and send it home. The Navy wasn't going to let me wear their clothes off the base, so the Marine officer and I had to go to the shipping area and try to get my clothes back.

"It was really funny, me and this officer digging through a big mound of bags looking for my name so I could go with him. After about an hour I finally found it … had to strip down to my skivvies and then put my old clothes and shoes on. Then we went to the Marine Corps Recruit Depot and I was issued all Marine clothes. I reported to my unit and started training the next day.

"Another funny thing happened during boot camp ... had a Navajo with a strange name, General Miles ... drove the Marines crazy trying to get his paperwork right. Every morning for about three days an officer would come into the bunkhouse and shout: 'General Miles! General Miles!' Guys were leaping up trying to salute, then he would stand up and answer 'present' and off they would go. The other guys got so mad that they had jumped up and tried to salute a 'general.'"

We were both laughing. "I can see where the Corps might have had a problem with a *PFC* General Miles." I said.

"After graduation, I went to the code school," he continued. "During the day, I taught the other Navajos how to repair their radios. Stayed up late into the night learning about it from the instructors. I understood Navajo better than I spoke it, so I became more of a field interpreter for my commanding officer. On Iwo, the action was so fast that my officer didn't always want to wait to receive a printed message, so I just told him what it said on the spot. My discharge papers actually say 'Interpreter 642.'"

"Did you ever see Philip Johnston?" I asked.

"Yeah, he hung around a lot when we were on break, tried to talk to us in Navajo, but it was hard to understand him, cause he'd get his verbs all messed up. Then sometime in July, he just disappeared. Never saw him again," Paul replied.

He spoke about his time on Iwo and what he did after the war, and then a knock on the door gave me an opportunity to interview another code talker: Merrill Sandoval.

MERRILL SANDOVAL

I put the tape recorder on "pause" and introduced myself. Seems Merrill got curious when I drove up to Paul's house. He lived next door and decided to find out what was going on. He asked Paul what we were up to, and Paul explained who I was and what I was doing.

With little ado, he began telling me he served in the second all-Navajo platoon with his brother Samuel. They were both assigned to the 5th Division and told me some very interesting details about the Navajo radio network. The time they spent in the code school was hard. Test day was difficult but when they got the hang of it, it started to get easier to learn and memorize.

"In combat we always knew where everyone was. We recognized each other's voices and we became so familiar we could finish writing down the message and hand it off before it was finished being relayed." Merrill said. "There was great power in our transmissions. I always felt secure hearing and using my language. The commanders were always amazed at what we did, could never figure out how it worked, but it did and they used it. Drove the Japs crazy."

Three and a half hours had passed, and both of these men had given me wonderful information not only about the code, but how they used it in combat, along with personal stories. I packed up my materials, thanked both of them for their service during the war, and promised to keep in touch. The drive back to Gallup proved to be calming, especially after nearly six hours of hearing about war and death. I couldn't wait to call Mary and tell her what I had learned. We had a great talk and I was ready to head home. It was only a two-hour drive to Albuquerque where I had an appointment with a code talker, another member of "The First 29" who lived in Albuquerque.

ANONYMOUS

Before I left Gallup, I called the code talker to make sure he remembered our appointment. He said to come at the appointed time and looked forward to meeting with me. His house was easy enough to find and I knocked on the door. His grandson answered and let me in.

I explained what I was doing and asked permission to record his story. He began his story like the code talkers before him with the Long Walk. I sat there, mesmerized by this retelling. He spoke as if it had happened yesterday and he was one of the survivors. Then he spoke about his experiences during boot camp.

"Boot camp was a strange experience, but it was good that we were all together. Eugene had some experience with the military and he taught the rest of us what to expect and how to conduct ourselves. I really enjoyed the firing range—never had a gun that big, just a squirrel gun on the rez. The drill sergeants were big, rough, and mean but they couldn't find tough enough drills we couldn't do with ease. We were all raised on Navajo land, didn't have modern things like running water and lights and we walked every day for miles. We were already tough."

He went on to tell me about his combat experience on Guadalcanal and it was chilling, to say the least. He didn't appear to be uncomfortable telling it, but it was clearly painful nonetheless. We had spent about an hour and a half going over the creation of the code and other events. At the end, I asked him to sign a release so I could use parts of what he told me. This was a problem.

"I can't sign this," he said. I was stunned. All of the other code talkers had signed without hesitation.

"May I ask why you can't sign it?" I asked.

He sat there for a few minutes deep in thought, then said, "At the end of the war, I was told by my commanding general to never talk about the code or how it was used. He made me solemnly swear and I did. Until today, I have never spoken about the war or what I did."

I pulled out the copy of the Navajo Dictionary, showed him the declassification stamp, and explained that it was okay for him to talk about it. He shook his head and sighed.

"That's interesting, but I still can't sign that release. I gave my word of honor never to talk about it. How do I declassify my word of honor?"

I had no answer for that. Then I did something, even though I wasn't sure how it would play out. "How about this—I give you my word of honor that what you told me will remain anonymous, that I will never reveal your name if you sign the release. This way I can still use what you told me, but no one will ever know you gave it to me." He signed the release and I thanked him for his service during the war and his hospitality. As I left to go to my cousin Kitty Brown's house, tears were streaking down my face. I pulled over and let them fall. I was overwhelmed with this man's deep sense of honor. I pulled myself together and headed for her house. Over the course of the many trips to the rez, she had welcomed me, Melinda, Mom, and Beth to stay with her on our way to and from Gallup. It broke up the trip into more manageable hours and she learned about the code talker story as it unfolded. This particular code talker story would be one I would not share with her, Carl, Mary, Zonnie, or anyone in my family.

On the way home, I started thinking about all the transcribing and collating this new information was going to entail, and how intense the process would become. However, it would all be worth it to get the true picture of the service the code talkers rendered during the war. I felt a great deal of satisfaction for what I had accomplished so far. I didn't know then how daunting a task putting this story together would be.

CHAPTER 11

THE PROCESS BEGINS

AFTER I GOT HOME, I fell into a routine: working, taking care of Melinda, then organizing and writing the story on the weekends. I color-coordinated everything so I could match code talkers to specific battles with relevant documents. I managed to amass 575 individual military documents, 35 code talker interviews, and 14 folders regarding the South Pacific campaigns. I had always been an organized person, but I had to become the Empress of Organization to put all this material in a comprehensive form.

I also had to find a Marine that could help explain some of the decisions surrounding the recruitment and use of the Navajos. I thought about contacting J. P. Berkeley, as he had been involved with so many early meetings regarding the code talkers. I called him and we had an extremely productive session.

"Mr. Berkeley, thank you for taking the time to speak with me. I have a few questions I need clarification on and if you can assist me, I would be ever so grateful," I said.

"Hum, well that depends on what you need to know and if I have the answer. So fire away," he said.

"Okay," I began. "Can you tell me why the Commandant would need to be informed of every Navajo recruit?"

"Well," he said, "I'm pretty sure that because he authorized the Pilot Project, and it turned out so successful, that he had to know how many Navajos were on hand. This was a 'Secret' project and when recommendations from commanders came in as to how many code talkers should be assigned to each division, he had to know the exact number on hand."

That made sense. "Do you have any idea where I might find the code school records?" I asked.

There was a short pause before he answered. "Didn't you find them in the archives?"

"No, I haven't been able to locate them anywhere," I said.

"Well, that certainly is strange. Can't imagine they would have tossed them. Sorry, but I don't have a clue," he said.

Damn! "Well, thanks for your input." I said. At this point I didn't feel that having the code school records would make that big of a difference to the story. Perhaps I would be able to locate them at a later time. With the advice from my sister Dona, I decided to begin the story with the retelling of the Long Walk. I wanted the reader to understand some history about the Navajo people and how the enforced acculturation affected the men who later became code talkers.

The next chapter would deal with The Empire of Japan and what led up to the bombing of Pearl Harbor. This would set the tone for every battle the Marines and code talkers were engaged in. The following chapters would be done in chronological order beginning with how the Marine Corps initiated the Pilot Project, the recruitment of "The First 29," and how they created the code.

Dissecting each battle was emotionally draining. The action was so brutal, so deadly, and so bloody, it often made it hard for me to sleep at night, especially Iwo Jima. Incorporating what the code talkers were doing with the battle action was sometimes really confusing. When Dona proofed the chapter on Iwo she told me that halfway through the battle I apparently lost track of an entire set of code talkers. One minute they were there and the next few paragraphs they disappeared! *Crap!* It took me two days to figure out how I lost track of them, find them, and put them back in the story. Okinawa would prove just as difficult.

PHILIP JOHNSTON

Zonnie called me in late April with information about Philip Johnston. Apparently he donated a bucket load of papers to the Museum of Northern Arizona and we thought it would be a good idea to investigate them. Frankly, I needed a break from the book, and there were still unanswered questions about what Johnston did or did not contribute to the code or the code school.

I arranged a quick trip the next week and met Zonnie at her parent's house. She and the boys had moved in with Carl and Mary after graduation, and we were going to drive down to Flagstaff the next day. We had no idea what Johnston's collection would reveal, but I dearly hoped some answers would be found.

Checking in at the museum, we requested the Philip Johnston papers. Zonnie and I divided them and began combing through them. As I read what he saved, I began to get the distinct impression that this man had a huge ego and was extremely disappointed he hadn't been given the proper credit for his demonstration. He had to literally beg the Marine Corps to let him join and all they granted him was a certain rank and designated him to be the liaison between the Navajo instructors and the commanding officers.

I turned the next page and gasped! Staring at me was a copy of a test paper, but there was *no* declassification stamp on it. *Oh My God! He stole it!* I nudged Zonnie and showed it to her, indicating the missing declassification stamp and she stared at it for a few minutes. "Seems like Johnston had sticky fingers," she said. I set it aside to make a copy and found fifteen more just like it. Then I found a copy of an article regarding Johnston's return to the City of Los Angeles dated late March 1945.

I remembered Paul Blatchford saying Johnston disappeared in July 1944, the same time the *Arizona Highways* article came out and the subsequent investigation. I surmised that because of the breach of security and his confession of the court-martial to Martin Link, that he may have been under some type of confinement or arrest from July 1944 to March 1945. Zonnie and I wondered what the Marine Corps might have done to Johnston if they'd known he was copying and stealing test papers from a "Secret" program.

When we got back to Carl and Mary's, we showed them what we'd found and discussed the possible consequences of Johnston's possible thievery. This quick trip had been very valuable and informative, but I had to get back to the task at hand.

BACK TO THE PROCESS

The entire story took me over a year to complete. Along the way, my sister Dona was gracious enough to read, edit, and comment on the story, and I could not have put it together without her assistance. When it was finished, Mom suggested I give it to a friend of hers who owned a publishing company for evaluation and recommendation. Up to this point I hadn't spent one moment thinking about what company would be publishing *Navajo Weapon*. I guess I believed someone would be as excited about this story as I was and publishing it wouldn't be a problem. For once, I was right.

Rik and Judy Rydlun owned Books Beyond Borders, a publishing company in Boulder, Colorado. I gave them the manuscript and two weeks later, Judy called me with her opinion.

"This is an incredible story," she said. "I had no idea the code talkers used their language during World War II. You have done a great job telling a comprehensive and intriguing tale."

"Thank you," I said. "Do you have any suggestions as to what type of publisher I should send a query letter to?" I asked.

"We want to publish it," she said. I was stunned.

"You do?" I said.

"Absolutely. We would be delighted to publish this book. Can you come in and meet with us this week?" she asked.

"I can come in after work on Thursday," I said.

The meeting on Thursday was a real eye-opener. Rik and Judy were wonderful people and their enthusiasm about this story matched mine. We began working out the details of a contract and after it was signed, I felt like I was walking on air. Everything had come together so well that I knew it wasn't just coincidence, but greater forces at work that made this all possible.

The next four months were spent laying out the book, editing, and making sure all the footnotes were correct. It was an intense process to say the least. This is when another dream about Iwo with Native American drumming and singing reoccurred.

DEEP IN THE DARK

I woke up around three in the morning with the sounds of drumming and singing still swirling in my head. I turned on the light and tried to clear my head. Then it came to me. One night back in 1978, when I was working in Ogden, Utah, I agreed to give a ride to four Native Americans. I couldn't tell you if they were Ute, Navajo, or some other tribe. They all had long waist-length hair and were dressed in camouflage clothing that was popular at the time, and were eager to get where they were going.

In all my years of living in many places I had never, ever given a ride to a hitchhiker. They needed to get to Salt Lake City and since it was on my way home, I mindlessly agreed. Just as we got on Interstate 80, it began to rain and the four men began to sing in a language I didn't recognize or understand, but it was hauntingly beautiful. The one in the front passenger seat turned to me and said, "Rain is always a blessing." I had never heard that saying before, but it made sense.

The rain stopped as we approached the highway interchange and the lights gave the misty area an orange sherbet color, and they asked to be dropped off near an exit. They exited the car and disappeared into the night. I drove home to Magna, not fully comprehending what had transpired. I had forgotten this incident, but the sense memory of hearing those four Native Americans singing must have been buried deep in my memory and going back over the intense battle on Iwo Jima brought it back to life.

I was so disturbed by this memory that I mentioned it to Rik and Judy. They listened to my recollection and said they were going to Trinidad, Colorado, to see Megan Garcia, one of their Native American authors, and were willing to ask her what the significance of that event might mean. I really wanted an explanation, so I gave them permission to relate the events to her. When they returned from their trip, they had plenty to tell me and it was really interesting and sort of spooky.

Judy told me the following: "When I spoke with Megan about your experience, she said she had a friend who was a shaman and would ask him to meditate on it and if there was something to tell, he would relay it before we left. Right before we set out to return home, this shaman came by and said: 'Tell your friend that those four men were messengers and that she was one of those that did not survive the battle. This is her chance to tell a similar story.'"

I sat there in absolute stunned silence. Then I found my voice and asked, "Let me understand, are you saying this shaman thinks I lived a past life, was involved in the battle on Iwo Jima and didn't survive, and that is why the code talker story came to me?"

"That's what it sounds like to us," Judy said.

I started to laugh, because this was *so* absurd. I believe in a lot of things, but having a past life as a Marine was not one I had *ever* remotely entertained. Now, you may pooh-pooh this, and I certainly did for a long time, but it may possibly explain how and why the code talker story came to me. Nothing else I have ever examined comes close to explaining it, so why not this?

"Well," I said. "It certainly is something to ponder."

REVIEWS AND COMMENTS

We decided that a galley copy of the book would be submitted to the Marine Corps. Since this was part of their history, it was essential we get their approval.

Michael Levatino, Books Beyond Borders' publicist, began formulating who would review the book and where book signings would take place. I gave him the addresses of *Leatherneck* magazine, Lee Cannon, and R. G. Rosenquist to name a few. This seemed to be happening so fast. It was hard to comprehend that after six years, the book was finally going to become a reality.

In March of 1994, the final edit of the manuscript was completed, and I had to create the index and check, then recheck the spelling of every name and place in the manuscript. I also began planning a banquet for the code talkers, where I would present the book to them. Mary and Carl were really pleased and excited about finally seeing the code talker story in print. Mary sent me a new list of current code talkers' and surviving relatives' addresses and I began inquiries about where and when to hold the banquet.

I contacted the Best Western in Gallup and arranged for the banquet to take place the day before the Inter-Tribal Indian Ceremonial in August. It would be the perfect time for this gathering and I hoped the code talkers would show up. I sent out over three hundred invitations at the beginning of June and the replies slowly started to stream in. If a code talker had passed away, and a number of them had, I sent the invitation to his widow or children. I arranged for Vincent Craig, son of code talker Bob Etsitty Craig, to perform his song, "My Daddy Was a Code Talker," and the hotel agreed to tape the entire ceremony.

I also invited Richard Bonham, who would be a surprise for Bill Toledo. My entire family would also attend. Henry and Alice couldn't come, but they would be sent a copy of the book. Books would also be sent to Tom Randant, J. P. Berkeley, Loren Myring, and Lee Cannon. Everything was coming together, and I couldn't wait to give the code talkers their story.

BANQUET DAY

In July, Rik and Judy asked me to stop by their office after work. I arrived and they had me sit down and close my eyes, then they put something in my hands. I opened my eyes to see the book. "This is the first copy off the press and it's for you," Judy said. I sat there staring at it for what seemed a long time. It was surreal. Here was the physical manifestation of six years of hard work. I carefully opened it and started to thumb through it. "This is the most beautiful thing I have ever seen," I said. "Well, next to my daughter of course." We all laughed and talked and couldn't wait for the day of the banquet and the trip down to Gallup.

Code Talker Banquet, Gallup, New Mexico, 1994.

ABOVE: *Mike Kiyaani.*

LEFT: *Sam Billison, Tom Begay, and Nina Begay.*

Code Talker Banquet, Gallup, New Mexico, 1994.

ABOVE: *Lemuel Yazzie (left) and Alfred Neuman (right) with their wives.*

RIGHT: *(left to right) John Goodluck, Teddy Draper, and John Kinsel.*

OPPOSITE TOP: *(left to right) Sharon Toledo, Richard Bonham, Sally McClain, and Bill Toledo.*

OPPOSITE BOTTOM: *(left to right) Teddy Draper and Sam Billison sign copies of* Navajo Weapon.

August 6, 1994 was fast approaching and I could only hope that everything would go off without a hitch. Rik, Judy, and Michael would be bringing the 230 books for the code talkers with them and I would take the list of attendees and start personalizing the books. Melinda volunteered to call out the code talker names while I presented the men or their representatives with the book. She took the list of names and we ran through them to make sure she pronounced them correctly.

On the day of the banquet, I set up three storyboards with photographs from the book and a place at the check-in table for the books to be signed by the code talkers for the President, the Commandant of the Marine Corps, and the Raider Association. I had been invited to attend the 50th Anniversary reunion of the Raider Battalions, which would take place in Las Vegas in September. There, I would present the books for the Raiders and the Commandant and I also would take one for their auction to raise money for the Raider charities.

Over 230 people were now seated in the banquet room. I had greeted almost all of them and was deeply pleased to see familiar faces again. Mary, Carl, Harold, Bill, Kee and Vincent Craig were seated at the head table. Everyone had been served their food and the room buzzed with chatter. Judy gave a welcome speech, introducing herself, Rik, and Michael. She then introduced Vincent Craig and he performed his song while people were eating. When the plates were cleared, I rose to address the attendees. To the best of my recollection, my speech went something like this:

"Good afternoon and thank you all for attending this very special event. My name is Sally McClain and I am here to present a very special tribute to the Navajo code talkers. Over the last six years, I have researched the archives and interviewed many in this room to put together the story of the service the Navajo code talkers rendered during the South Pacific Campaigns of World War II.

"This journey was also aided by many people who either served with the code talkers or had knowledge of their program. Many others, relatives included, provided invaluable inspiration and advice during this process. As I call your names, would you please stand and be acknowledged: My father, Navy veteran of the South Pacific Don McClain, my mother Lee Redfield, my sisters Beth McClain and Dona McClain, brother Fred McClain, my daughter Melinda McClain, Mary Gorman, my publishers Rik and Judy Rydlun, special guest vocalist Vincent Craig, and Richard Bonham.

"Now, without further ado, I have the great privilege and honor to present *Navajo Weapon* to the United States Marine Corps Navajo code talkers."

Melinda began calling out the names in alphabetical order and I went around the room, presenting the book and thanking each man for his service during the war. By the end of the banquet, I set aside books for the few code talkers that did not show. I would mail them after I returned home. The attendees began looking through the book, and the room became full of happy chatter. They were asking each other to sign their books, and I was gathering as many signatures for my copy as I could. It was a fantastic day and I couldn't have been more pleased with the attendance, outcome, and the graciousness of everyone present.

Back in my room, with all of my family in tow, Rik and Judy opened a bottle of champagne to toast our success, and Michael presented me with the first review of the book from the *Gallup Independent* newspaper. He also informed me that I had a space to sell the book during the ceremonial and would leave me with a case of books. Then we ordered pizza and spent the rest of the evening reliving the success of the banquet and the book.

After Melinda went to sleep I sat up and marveled at the book that took six years to come to fruition. It still seemed surreal—now I was a published author and even though I didn't know what that was supposed to feel like, the pleasant euphoria I was bathing in felt just right. I couldn't wait for the public to have access to this story, so the code talkers could take their rightful place in not only Navajo and American history, but World War II and Marine Corps history as well.

During the ceremonial, many children of code talkers who'd passed away came to thank me for the book. They gave me wonderful tokens and I felt honored and humbled by their gifts. On the second day of the ceremonial, I met a woman who would astound me with a story about the code talkers.

Jacqueline came up to where I was selling *Navajo Weapon* and asked in a very thick French accent if this was a book about the code talkers. "Yes," I replied.

"I want to tell you something. I worked with the Intelligence in the French Underground during the war. I knew all about them and I'm glad the rest of the world will know about them, too," she said.

I was stunned! *The French Underground knew about the code talkers?* "That's remarkable," I said. "How did you know about them? Why would you know about them?"

She smiled and said, "My dear, anyone who was Intelligence knew all about codes and the Navajo was one we knew the Japanese and the Germans would never be able to figure out. It was quite amusing, very clever of the Americans to use a native language to defeat their enemy." She bought a copy, I personalized it for her, and she left.

Of all the unexpected things that happened around the code talker story, meeting this woman who was a member of the French Underground took first prize for astounding me. It gave me goose bumps thinking that Winston Churchill might have been privy to the Navajo Dictionary, and dare I say … Stalin? I would probably never know if they did or not, but it was fascinating to think about.

The ceremonial turned out to be a fairly successful venue for selling the book and I ended up taking home ten books out of forty. Carl and Mary came by on the last day and thanked me once again for the banquet and the book. "I couldn't have done it without your friendship, advice, and support. I'll miss these trips to the rez," I said.

"Well," Mary said, "just because the book is done, doesn't mean we won't see each other again. Rik and Judy asked us to go to Texas, so Carl can give lectures to some of the colleges and have a book signing afterwards."

"Wow! That sounds like fun. They haven't spoken to me about that yet, but count me in," I said. We hugged and said our goodbyes and I was thrilled with the prospect of traveling around Texas with Carl and Mary. We had all become so close over the last six years. Carl and Mary had become like a second set of parents to me, and spending more time with them would be a real treat.

The trip home from the Ceremonial was filled with pleasant memories. It still hadn't sunk in that I was a legitimate published author, but over the next few months, I became very comfortable with this label. I thought back to that first phone call with Harold and everything it set in motion. To this day, I still do not quite understand why the code talker story came to me and there may never be a logical answer to that question. I will always be grateful to whatever higher power put me on that path. I met and came to know people I would never have had the opportunity to encounter otherwise, and it changed not only me, but my entire family, in ways that are still being measured. That turned out to be the greatest gift of all.

EPILOGUE

DURING THE SEARCH FOR THE NAVAJO CODE TALKERS, I uncovered a great many heretofore-unknown aspects about their service, and some I still have no answers for. I was unable to locate the code school records, which would have given me a list of every Navajo who was certified as a code talker. I suspect that the Office of Naval Intelligence (ONI) may have them in their old World War II records, but to date I have been unable to locate them.

I was also unable to locate any Marine Corps document stating when the code school was closed, if indeed it ever was. I did find a document that had a code talker, William Kien, listed as 642 for deployment to Korea. He would neither confirm nor deny that he used the code after World War II. I was unable to locate the military record for Philip Johnston, so the question of exactly what happened that led to his court-martial went unanswered.

I never found "official" proof that bodyguards for the code talkers were ever officially ordered, or that the Navajo Dictionary was used in any other conflict past World War II. But I did discover the reason for their exclusion in World War II books. Because their code was not declassified until 1969, the majority of books and movies were already finished, and those authors and filmmakers had no knowledge of their role. That was the only reason for the exclusion.

The Navajos created a code that would never be broken. It is a masterpiece that deserves an honored place in museums. A copy of the code is displayed in the CIA Museum, and a National Navajo Code Talkers Museum is planned to be built in Window Rock, Arizona.

After the book was published, I made copies of every document and interview and donated them to the following institutions: The Navajo Community College, the Navajo Tribal Museum, Camp Pendleton archives, and the Marine Corps University Library in Quantico, Virginia. I felt it was my duty to make this material available not only to the Navajo people, but to the Marine Corps that the code talkers love and honor to this day.

PERSONAL NOTES

EUGENE ROANHORSE CRAWFORD, HAROLD FOSTER, WILSIE BITSIE, AND Dean Wilson passed away in 1996 and 1997 and it broke my heart. All of these gentle, honorable souls generously gave me their time and their personal stories for the book and I will never forget that. Harold's son Larry wrote me a wonderful letter after his father passed away and thanked me for telling his story in the book. He also said, "Dad instructed us to do something very peculiar around his grave. He is buried at the Fort Defiance Military Cemetery and told us to outline his grave with twenty-nine stones. Do you have any idea what it means?" His letter went on to say that Harold died from an enlarged heart. It gave out before any help could arrive, but he died working with the health agency he loved so much. I cried many tears at this loss. Harold might have been a little gruff around the edges, but he was instrumental in revealing the code talker story.

Wow! I was stunned but I most certainly did know what the stones meant. I called Larry the day I received his letter and told him the significance of his father's "peculiar" request. "Larry," I said, "first let me say how sorry I am for your loss. Your father was the first code talker I met, and the book would not have been possible without his contribution. Now, I think the reason he requested the twenty-nine stones is that they represent The First 29 code talkers. When I first met him he told me he didn't believe that The First 29 created the first code, which made it possible for other Navajos to be used in this way. I believe he finally came to the conclusion that The First 29 did create the first code and this was his way of paying tribute to them. Does that make sense?"

"Yeah, it does," he said. "I always wondered why he seemed so reluctant to believe The First 29, I guess your book finally convinced him." I'm glad it did.

The death of Carl Nelson Gorman in 1998 almost killed me. Carl was the most intriguing, generous, funny, loving, artistic, spiritual, honorable human being I have ever had the privilege to know. He and Mary were the second-most important catalysts for the code talker story and without them there would have been no book. Losing him was like losing a parent—the wound was deep and almost unbearable. Mary passed away September 9, 2001, and I still feel her loss. I will always cherish the time I spent with Carl and Mary and will love and honor them all the days of my life.

After Mary's service, a group of about twenty code talkers were huddled in a circle and talking in a hushed tone. I was so curious about what they were discussing that I eavesdropped. What I heard reinforced everything I knew, admired, and respected about the code talkers.

Just days after 9/11, they were talking about how to charter a bus to Camp Pendleton. They were really upset about the unprovoked attack on New York City and the Pentagon and they were going to present themselves to the camp commander and offer their services as code talkers. One of them remarked, "Don't think any Arab knows Navajo."

They never went, but I would have loved to be a fly on the wall if the Camp Pendleton commander heard a bunch of eighty-plus-year-old veterans offering to resurrect their code against terrorists.

Over the years, many code talkers have passed away, and it always hurts my heart when I hear of their passing. It will truly be the saddest day of all when they are gone. I travel to Lake Powell almost every year and have the privilege of giving lectures alongside three or four code talkers. It's always rewarding to visit with them, catch up on all the news, and see the public's reaction to them even after all these years. They always amaze me and I will be in awe of them until the day I cross to the other side. May they and their many generations to come walk in beauty all the days of their lives.

ACKNOWLEDGMENTS

I WOULD LIKE TO TAKE THIS OPPORTUNITY to thank everyone I encountered during the search for the Navajo code talkers. Their remarkable story could not have been recorded for history without their contributions. With love, honor, and respect I name the following contributors:

Carl, Mary, and Zonnie Gorman, Harold Foster, Eugene Crawford, Wilsie Bitsie, Tom Begay, Bill Toledo, Kee Etsicitty, Teddy Draper, John Kinsel, John Goodluck, Dean Wilson, Paul Blatchford, Merril Sandoval, Sam Billison, Richard Bonham, Henry and Alice Hisey, Tom Randant, R. G. Rosenquist, Loren Myring, and J. P. Berkeley.

SUGGESTED READING

Kawano, Kenji. *Warriors: Navajo Code Talkers.* New York: Cooper Square Publishing, 1990.

Mack, Stephen. *It Had to Be Done: The Navajo Code Talkers Remember World War II.* Tucson: Whispering Dove Design, 2008.

McClain, Sally. *Navajo Weapon: The Navajo Code Talkers.* Tucson: Rio Nuevo Publishers, 2002.

Nez, Chester, and Judith Schiess Avila. *Code Talker: The First and Only Memoir by One of the Original Code Talkers of WWII.* New York: Berkley, 2011.

Paul, Doris A. *The Navajo Code Talkers, 25th Anniversary Edition.* Pittsburgh: Dorrance Publishing Co. Inc., 1998.

Tohe, Laura, and Deborah O'Grady. *Code Talker Stories.* Tucson: Rio Nuevo Publishers, 2012.

PHOTO CREDITS

Kenji Kawano: *back cover; pages 12, 23, 43, 90.*

Brian Leddy: *front cover; pages ii–iii, photo of medal this page and throughout book.*

Sally McClain: *pages 26, 50, 59, 62, 74, 78, 96, 109–111.*

INDEX

A

Albuquerque, New Mexico, 73, 100
Arizona Highways magazine, 58, 89, 105
Arlington National Cemetery, 53–54

B

Begay, Tom, 27, 28, 109
Benally, John, 15, 28, 42, 69
Berkeley, J. P., 65, 103, 108
Bernstein, Jerry, 49, 50, 54
Bernstein, Susan, 49, 50, 54
Billison, Sam, 67, 77, 78, 109, 110
Bitsie, Wilsie, 26, 29, 39, 46, 67, 80, 85, 87, 94, 117
Blatchford, Paul, 67, 80, 85, 87, 94, 98–99, 105, 119
Bonham, Richard, 62, 64, 78, 108, 110, 112,
Bosque Redondo, 22, 74, 79
Bougainville, 28, 53, 63, 71, 72, 73, 75
Boulder, Colorado, 5, 11, 25, 106
Brown, Kitty, 101
Bureau of Indian Affairs (BIA), 58, 60, 65, 75, 88

C

Camp Elliott, 37
Camp Pendleton, 63, 94, 115, 118
Cannon, Lee, 108
Canyon de Chelly, 74, 95, 97
Carlson, Evans F., 44, 92
Choctaw, 51–52

Cohoe, James, 61, 84
Combat Team 28, 82, 95
Craig, Bob Etsitty, 108
Craig, Vincent, 108, 112
Crawford, Eugene Roanhorse, 26, 28, 39, 41, 43–46, 117

D

Draper, Teddy, 61, 80, 83, 84, 85, 94–98, 110, 111
Draper, Teddy Junior, 97
Duke, Doris, 80, 84–85

E

Empire of Japan, 48, 104
Etsicitty, Kee, 71–73

F

Fort Defiance, 12, 24, 35, 117
Fort Wingate, 36
Foster, Harold, 8, 9–19, 79–80, 117
French Underground, 113–114

G

Gallup Inter-Tribal Indian Ceremonial, 61, 67, 79–80, 85, 108, 113–114
Gallup, New Mexico, 8, 11, 13, 14, 18–19, 24–25, 27, 39, 43, 61, 67, 85, 89, 98, 100
Ganado, Arizona, 35
GI Bill, 78
Gorman, Carl, 16–19, 21–27, 31–34, 36–41, 52, 53, 87–89, 114, 117–118

Gorman, Mary, 21–27, 31–34, 36–41, 67, 87–89, 114, 117–118
Gorman, R. C., 13, 16
Gorman, Zonnie, 46–54, 104–105
Guadalcanal, 41, 45, 53, 92, 100
Guam, 28, 63, 64, 71, 73, 76, 92, 93

H

Haskie, Ross, 42
Hawaii, 77, 94
Hayes, Ira, 49, 50, 53, 92–93
Hisey, Henry, 61–62
Hisey, Alice, 61–62
Hubbell Trading Post, 35

I

Iwo Jima, 10–11, 17, 28, 38, 53, 63, 64, 70, 71, 72, 76, 78, 79, 81–83, 87, 92, 95, 97, 99, 104, 106–107

J

Johnston, Philip, 19, 25–26, 38–39, 57–58, 88–89, 92, 94, 97, 99, 104–105, 115

K

Kinsel, John, 27–29, 111

L

Laguna, New Mexico, 73, 76
Laguna tribe, 73, 76
Leatherneck magazine, 61, 108
Levatino, Michael, 108
Link, Martin, 89, 105

M

Manuelito, Johnny, 15, 28, 75
Maori, 45
Marine Corps Historical Center, 7, 21, 54, 56
Marine Corps Memorial, 54
Marine Corps Recruit Depot, 36–37, 98
McClain, Beth, 1, 3, 101, 112

McClain, Dona, 11, 13, 104, 105
McClain, Melinda, 1, 25, 30, 35–36, 40–41, 67, 112–113
Miles, General, 99
Museum of Northern Arizona, 104–105
Myring, Loren, 64

N

National Archives, 39, 46, 51–53,
Navajo Dictionary, 59, 101, 114, 115
Navy Recruit Depot, 98
New Zealand, 45
Notah, Willie, 64

O

Okinawa, 38, 104

P

Pearl Harbor, 89, 104
Phoenix, Arizona, 5, 46
Pilot Project, 48, 58, 65, 103, 104
Pima, 50
Price, Wilson, 42

R

Raider Battalions, 29, 39, 44, 46, 66, 70, 72, 92–93, 112
Randant, Tom, 65, 108
Rosenquist, R. G., 66, 108
Route 66, 11, 13, 25, 39
Rydlun, Judy, 106, 112
Rydlun, Rik, 106, 112

S

Saipan, 37, 53, 89, 93
Sandoval, Merrill, 99–100
Sandoval, Samuel, 99
Shinn, Frank, 36, 48
SRH 120, 51–52, 54
Suitland Archives, 53, 55–60, 81–83
Suitland, Maryland, 55, 56, 62

T

Tarawa, 15, 16
The First 29, 19, 25, 26, 29, 35–48, 80, 100,
    104, 117
Toledo, Bill, 27, 62–63, 73–76, 111
Toledo, Preston, 28, 75
Treaty of 1868, 14, 23, 39, 40, 47, 48, 91

U

University of Utah, 80, 84–85

V

Vanderwagen, New Mexico, 71
Vogel, Clayton B., 58, 65

W

Washington, D. C., 39, 46, 48, 49, 54, 55, 81,
    84
Wilson, Dean, 27, 29, 31, 117
Window Rock, Arizona, 13, 14, 35, 115

Y

Yazzie, Felix, 42–43

ABOUT THE AUTHOR

SALLY McCLAIN, author of *Navajo Weapon*, loves finding a missing piece of history and bringing it to light. Over the past fifteen years Sally has spoken about the Code Talkers at veterans organizations, schools, and universities. Her next book is *A Taint on Texas*, about a Native American struggle for land that culminated in a massacre. She lives in Broomfield, Colorado.

Left to right: Wilford Buck, Keith Little, Sally McClain, Samuel Tso, Alfred Peaches, and Albert Smith at Lake Powell, 2007.